D0280396

the complete guide to
renovating
& improving
your property

the complete guide to

renovating
& improving
your property

2ND EDITION

liz hodgkinson

KOGAN PAGE

London and Philadelphia

First published in Great Britain in 2004 by Kogan Page Limited
Second edition published in 2007

120 Pentonville Road
London N1 9JN
United Kingdom
www.kogan-page.co.uk

525 South 4th Street, #241
Philadelphia PA 19147
USA

© Liz Hodgkinson, 2004, 2007

ISBN-10   0 7494 4870 9
ISBN-13   978 0 7494 4870 7

Library of Congress Cataloging-in-Publication Data

Hodgkinson, Liz.
 The complete guide to renovating and improving your property /
   Liz Hodgkinson. -- 2nd ed. p. cm.
 Includes index.
 ISBN-13: 978-0-7494-4870-7
 ISBN-10: 0-7494-4870-9
 1. Dwellings--Maintenance and repair--Amateurs' manuals. I. Title.
 TH4817.3.H55 2007
 690'.80286--dc22   2006035072

British Library Cataloguing in Publication Data

A CIP record for this book is available from the British Library.

Typeset by Saxon Graphics Ltd, Derby
Printed and bound in Great Britain by Thanet Press Ltd, Margate

Contents

Introduction

The great home improvement frenzy

As I sit writing this, my front garden is tastefully decorated with an old washbasin and broken bathroom tiles. Next door's front garden is full of old doors, rotten planks, bags of cement and builders' rubble. Oh, a bath, sink and loo have just joined the heap.

Across the road, scaffolding has gone up. A few doors down, there is a house with (currently) no stairs, no floorboards and boarded-up windows. Opposite sits a large skip into which old washing machines, fridges, cookers, storage heaters and smashed windowpanes have been thrown. A sodden double mattress lies on the pavement.

Yes, it all looks terrible. However, even though my street might have the air of an abandoned, lawless inner-city estate, it is actually a desirable enclave undergoing intense gentrification. At any one time, at least half a dozen houses in my short street of just 22 dwellings are likely to be undergoing major renovation.

It's the same story in many parts of London. Investigative author Piers Paul Reid writes that his neighbourhood – upmarket Holland Park – is alive with 'the constant noise of builders' drills, stonecutters and cement mixers. There has not been a month in the past 20 years without some renovation going on in one or other of the houses in our street. Huge sums are paid for handsome houses in excellent condition which are then gutted after they change hands to provide new kitchens, bathrooms, conservatories or swimming pools in the basement. The noise is in stereo: the same sounds come from refurbishment of houses that face our garden.'

In my own slightly more downmarket area of London, a large, expensively refurbished house recently changed hands for upwards of £800,000. It was in immaculate condition, yet, less than a month after the new people moved in, all the costly additions were outside in the skip. The hand-built kitchen, decided the new owners, was *so* last year – or, to be more accurate, *so* four years ago, when the house was completely gutted and modernized.

Don't imagine, though, that this constant gutting and refurbishment takes place only in London's prime postcodes. Renovation and upgrading of homes has become a national pastime, even obsession. It has been largely fuelled by endless makeover shows on television that constantly raise consciousness and awareness of what can be done and give us ever grander and more ambitious ideas about home improvement.

Until I saw a series of glorious kitchen extensions on television, I was perfectly content with my own kitchen. Suddenly, though, it seemed small, dark and cramped, at least by contrast with the light, spacious, airy constructions featured in the programmes. It wouldn't do at all. It looked old-fashioned. It was a kitchen of yesteryear, poky, way behind the times. So of course I had to have a kitchen extension myself; the results were immortalized on Channel 4 in February, 2004.

Now I'm thinking, maybe the bathroom's a bit small and cramped as well. Is there any way of making it bigger, grander, more state of the art? What about a loft extension with en suite bathroom? The patio garden could do with being landscaped, too….

After all, my next door neighbour, who had an identical kitchen extension to mine at the same time, has just ripped his existing bathroom out to make way for a bigger, better and more modern version. I can hardly be left behind in the home improvement stakes, now can I?

When a friend moved to a small but very expensive two-bedroom Georgian cottage a couple of years ago, she instantly set about remodelling it completely. The builders have been in more or less permanent residence ever since. First of all she had a loft conversion, which gave her another bedroom and bathroom. Then she had an expensive wooden floor laid in the living room and two fireplaces put in. After that, the kitchen looked all wrong, so she had it totally remodelled into a vast kitchen diner. The existing units, plus the flooring and ceiling, had to be replaced at the same time. So it goes on.

Another couple of friends have just recently bought a quaint fisherman's cottage in Devon as a second home. They instantly embarked on a £100,000 renovation programme, which will take six months, at least, to complete. It is a major undertaking, especially as their main home is a good four hours' drive away. To embark on this project, they had to get planning permission, employ an architect and find reliable builders. Yet, they are doing it without turning a hair. How come? Simply because it is the fourth such project they have undertaken in the past 20 years. They, like many people today, have become old hands at the renovation game.

Instead of making frequent long trips to their uninhabitable new home, they could be putting their feet up and enjoying their retirement. Instead, the renovation bug has bitten them and they feel there is very little they can do about it, except to succumb.

Neither I, nor any of my friends and acquaintances who have undertaken these grand alterations and renovations, is a professional property developer. We are amateurs, whose standards and ideas just keep being raised all the time.

Those who find their home is suddenly too small are discovering – again thanks to scores of television programmes and the endless proliferation of makeover magazines – that they may be able to extend their existing place more or less indefinitely. One of my neighbours, with two small children, has had a loft extension, a conservatory extension, a second bathroom and the ceiling raised on a small bedroom – all this rather than face actually moving house and getting to know a new neighbourhood.

In many areas of the country these days, the skip, Portaloo, trade vans, cranes, scaffolding and front gardens full of rubble are all part of the permanent street scene. A nationwide frenzy of improvement, renovation, updating and extending is gripping us all.

Many factors have influenced the intense and ever-growing preoccupation with improving, updating, gutting and renovating. They are, I believe:

▌ the easy availability of remortgage money and loan facilities and increase in equity on the majority of properties, enabling finance to be raised for ever more ambitious building and renovation projects;

I   the endless television shows that are giving the viewing public ever more exotic home improvement ideas;

I   the development of power tools, which have brought ever more difficult jobs into the realm of the amateur;

I   the proliferation of hire shops, where you can hire large pieces of expensive equipment formerly reserved for the building trade;

I   the development of huge out-of-town DIY supermarkets, such as B&Q, Homebase and Wickes;

I   the way we live now meaning that everybody wants entertaining space, eat-in kitchens and en suite bathrooms and shower rooms;

I   fast-changing fashions and trends in interior decoration, meaning that styles and design ideas now date quickly;

I   the enormous influence of Feng Shui – the Eastern art of placement – giving people a new way of looking at their interiors;

I   the buy-to-let revolution, encouraging ever more people to buy properties as investments rather than just homes;

I   the rush to buy second and holiday homes ensuring that ever more people are now doing up not one, but several of their own properties;

I   high property prices, extremely high stamp duty and the enormous cost of moving are all encouraging more people to look at their existing homes to see if they can be improved and extended;

I   ever more people are now considering property development as a way of making money, rather than investing in pensions, stocks or shares;

I   the modernization of building technology, meaning that supporting walls can be knocked down, glass roofs constructed, ceilings raised or lowered and en suite bath-rooms fitted almost anywhere. Previously, these alterations would have been too daunting for ordinary people to contemplate;

▌ women have entered the home improvement, renovation, property development and building game and brought their own ideas to a previously all-male industry – it was not until women began to be earners and homeowners themselves that homes started to improve, as they have gone on improving ever since, as it was only when women had money of their own that stylish kitchens and beautiful bathrooms began to be fitted in even quite ordinary homes;

▌ the relatively easy availability of finance for home improve-ments, extensions, lofts, conservatories and kitchens has also fuelled the home improvement craze. There is fierce compe-tition among mortgage lenders and, if the lender believes the improvement will greatly add to the value and saleability of the property, then refinancing is usually simple. It is also possible to borrow money on credit cards to finance renova-tions and, although not recommended because of the high interest repayments, many people resort to this.

We are now well acquainted with building terms, as well. We all know about 'contingency', RSJs, stud walls, first fix, breeze blocks, dry lining and plasterboard. Indeed, we have all spent Sundays worshipping at today's cathedrals – the DIY warehouses – where we can see for ourselves what planks of timber, bags of plaster, power tools and bathroom fixtures look like. Knowledge and equipment once confined to the building trades have passed into the public domain.

Then, of course, the television programmes make it look so easy. On makeover shows, the job is done at the speed of a silent Charlie Chaplin film. In just half an hour, or less, a former wreck is converted into a stylish, spacious modern home complete with suitable 'staging', such as a vase of flowers, bowl of fruit, expensive olive oil and balsamic vinegar in the kitchen and terribly tasteful toiletries and fluffy towels in the bathroom(s).

It is certainly true that one of the great satisfactions in life is completing a really big and ambitious renovation project and then gasping in amazement at the results. In fact, it frequently happens that when I go to lunch or a dinner party, the first ice-breaking activity is for the guests to pore over architects' plans and drawings of front elevations, electrical circuits and so on. Before I even have a drink in my hand, my excited hosts will show me round their new extension, conservatory, loft room, kitchen or bathroom. Nor is this on a par with showing holiday slides – we dinner guests can't wait to see the refurbishments.

It is all extremely exciting but, as with most exciting projects, renovating your home – or, indeed, any property – can be an intensely stressful, high-risk activity. It is expensive and complicated and there is a lot that can go wrong.

This book shows you how to go about deciding on every aspect of property improvement, to make up your mind as to whether or not it is worth the effort, whether it will be a good investment and you are likely to make decent money out of the endeavour.

It also, most importantly, shows you how to get the very best out of a group of people who are becoming ever more a part of our daily lives: the builders. For without builders and their allied trades, no property renovation can ever happen.

Although my parents' generation rarely had the builders in, these days even quite small properties can be swarming with up to a dozen men at any one time. When an old friend called on me recently, I said, 'Come in, you're the eleventh man to arrive here this morning.' Also, these workmen are not robots; they are very human, with their own distinct personalities, likes and dislikes, moods and emotions – all of which the property owner has to take on board.

These days, your house may have one wall completely knocked down and its entire structure supported by a series of Acrows. In my garden, as I write, is an ever-turning cement mixer. In fact, when I had my extension done, the cement mixer was in the kitchen. Equipment once confined to large building sites is entering our homes and may live there for many months while we, the other residents, try to carry on normal life around it.

Builders are becoming ever more central to our lives and yet, when planning large-scale renovations and improvements, they are mostly forgotten about or shoved into the background. Get the relationship with these people wrong, though, and your world can literally come crashing down around your ears, taking all your money, hopes and dreams with it. If you fall out with your builders, they may well take umbrage and walk off site, leaving a heap of brickwork where your living room wall used to be.

Yes, property improvement can be daunting and traumatic. At the same time it is highly creative, tremendous fun and – when you get it right – adds to the quality of your life like nothing else. The pleasure that a successful renovation brings is endless and there are few satisfactions to beat putting the finishing touches to a lengthy, expensive and complicated refurbishment programme. If, into the bargain, you can hold a housewarming party to which your builders are cordially invited, then you know for sure that the whole thing has been a resounding success.

Part 1
Preparation

1 Is it worth it?

It is so easy to be bitten by the property development and home improvement bug that you can, if you are not very careful, find yourself embarking on large-scale, expensive renovation projects before you have really worked out whether or not they are a good idea and will genuinely add value.

Television makeover programmes make the whole thing look so seductive, inspiring and exciting that even people with heads normally as hard as a builder's hat can become carried away by a dream of making a tired, dated property look wonderful and then selling it immediately for a huge profit.

It seems irresistible, especially as most of the people featured on the TV programmes are 'ordinary' members of the public, people without special building expertise or knowledge. Before calling in a team of builders, though, you need to know for certain whether or not the enhancements you are planning are really, really worth it – from every point of view. Property development is a high-risk, high-cost and *very* high-stress undertaking, even when things go right, never mind when they go wrong.

So, whether you are contemplating renovating your own home, buying for investment, doing up a wreck, developing a property portfolio, building your own home from scratch or refurbishing a second or holiday home, bear the following factors in mind.

The true cost of renovation

Those of us who are addicted to television property shows – and 'real estate' shows are just as popular in the United States as the UK, so it's not just a British thing, by any means – have to be aware of the real cost of renovation. We are so used to watching people trying to do everything on a tiny budget and changing a room for just £500 that it's easy to imagine renovation is a doddle, in both cash and time.

The *real* average costs of home improvements (in 2006) are rather different:

▮   extending a side return costs between £20,000 and £30,000;

▮   converting a loft costs around £35,000, minimum;

▮   digging and tanking out a cellar comes in at anything from £75,000 to £200,000.

These prices do not include any redecoration or furnishing of the new rooms.

How much will it cost?

An absolute minimum for a new bathroom would be £4,000; for a kitchen, £5,000 – and these are prices for ordinary kitchens and bathrooms, not high-spec, state-of-the-art designer statements. Even just painting and decorating a single room could cost £1,000. Then there are curtains, flooring and walls to consider, so don't be fooled by those programmes where you are told that the 'budget' for the new kitchen is £897, or something just as daft.

Also, look very closely at the rundown of costs in makeover magazines. Very often they conveniently forget to put in the very high cost of labour, just mentioning the materials – as is the case in the *Changing Rooms* television show. How much would it cost to hire Linda Barker?

Before embarking on any major renovation, make sure that you are aware of the real costs of the work. It ain't cheap. Plus, it is always going to be a lot of hassle. The cost is not only financial – it can also shred your nerves to pieces.

If you are developing for profit, you also have to add on the cost of drawing up plans, obtaining planning permission, satisfying building regulations, undertaking soundproofing, putting in fire alarms and health and safety features, where applicable.

Then, it is always a good idea to cost in finishing touches, such as painting and decorating, carpets or other flooring, curtains and blinds, furniture, fireplaces and garden design, for example. There is nothing worse than a project that can't be properly finished because you have run out of money.

The state of the property market

This is the first thing to analyse closely, so you can be reasonably certain that you are not going to make a very expensive mistake. For, although a clean, well-presented property may sell more quickly than a rundown place, the difference in price may not be so great as you imagine. If people don't want it, they don't want it, however well you may have cleaned, staged and presented the property. Also, some locations are already overvalued, so whatever you do to a property in such an area won't add much, if anything.

Research

It is essential, when looking for the next big hotspot, to do thorough research beforehand, rather than hoping an area will come up just because you have bought there.

Estate agent Lucy Winfield, presenter of the UKTV show *Property Prophets*, has this advice:

> The first thing to look out for is skips in the street as this indicates that the process has at least started and incomers are spending money on their properties.
>
> When white gravel appears in the garden, window boxes are installed and plastic windows and doors are being replaced by wooden ones, you can be certain the area is on its way up. A uniform look in a street makes it much more desirable, rather than when everything is a nasty, cheap mishmash. Matching roofs also indicate an area being on the up.

Another small, but unmistakable, sign is when upmarket shops and supermarkets arrive in the area. The presence of a Lidl's might indicate the area is going down, whereas a Waitrose or a Marks and Spencer Simply Food means that the yuppies are moving in. If you see more upmarket newspapers and publications in your local newsagent – for instance, copies of the *Spectator* and *New Statesman* – you know the area is moving up.

The most significant aspect is the 'trickle effect' whereby an area next to an existing hotspot starts to come up. Areas subject to major government schemes, or where major developers are moving in, could also be coming hotspots. Plymouth, for instance, is in the middle of a major regeneration scheme, and Worthing on the South Coast is now attracting big development money after decades, even centuries, of being Brighton's ugly, unregarded sister. In Glasgow, there is a whole new media village and the Ibrox area is buzzing with trendy shops, boutiques and restaurants.

You should also look out for the appearance of new, high-quality restaurants and bars, and always make sure you drive slowly round the area to get a feel of it before taking the plunge.

Other pointers are neighbours and schools. You can get a neighbourhood profile online by going to www.upmystreet.com, which gives advice on matters ranging from neighbours' average incomes to the kind of newspapers they read. When large houses are being converted into flats, this usually means first-time buyers are entering the area and this will be the cue for new restaurants and bars to come to the area. Lots of noisy pubs can devalue an area, and these can be a nuisance at night. Neighbourhood associations will be able to provide information on such issues.

Parents of young children should check out which schools are doing well in league tables, and this can be accessed by going to www.dfes.gov.uk/performancetables. Ofsted at www.ofsted.gov.uk also has useful information on schools in the area. It is not a bad idea to drive or walk around when kids are coming out of school, to get an idea of the kind of children and parents attending the local schools. Also check out the area in the early evening to see whether gangs of kids are roaming around. The presence of very many 'To Let' signs may indicate that there are many tenants or housing associations in the area, and this may have an adverse effect on the value of your property, however much you spend on renovation.

All this may sound hideously snobbish, but it is a fact that some areas take decades to regenerate, and you may not have all the time in the world to wait.

Some examples of how to do it and how not to do it

When husband and wife team Nicola and Matthew Naish decided to become property developers, they first looked around in their home town of Hove. 'We soon realized that there was no way we could add value, as the properties were already so expensive', says Nicola. 'So we had to look further afield.' They chose Worthing – a seaside resort on the (very slow) up, but even here they had to be careful. 'We decided that East Worthing was not right and, in the end, there was only a tiny corner of West Worthing that we felt was coming up quickly and was suitable for the market we had in mind.'

Their gamble, in this instance, paid off, as all five of the flats that they created from a former five-bedroom house sold within the first week, at the full asking price.

Next, however, is an example of what not to do. A professional property developer and builder bought a rundown three-bedroom Victorian terraced house at auction for £450,000. The house needed total renovation and got it. The renovations took a year and cost £120,000. The developer hoped to sell the house for £650,000, which was the absolute ceiling price in that area for that type of property.

On paper, and on television, these figures might look quite impressive, giving as they do a massive £80,000 pre-tax profit. By the time you add on the estate agent's and lawyer's fees, capital gains tax (which you have to pay on any property apart from your own principal residence) and mortgage or loan repayments, it's not starting to look so good.

In fact, when you have taken these sums into account, the profit margin narrows to just £38,235. Here's how the figures stack up:

▌ £15,275 estate agent's fees;

▌ £1,000 legal fees;

▌ £25,490 capital gains tax;

giving a total bill of £41,765 – and these figures haven't even included loan repayments or stamp duty on the purchase.

'OK,' you might say, '£40,000 is still not a bad sum to make, after tax.' Yes, but – and here's the real problem – *the house didn't sell!* It remained on the market for months, with three different agents. In the end, the developer decided to rent it out, for £500 a week, which at least created a little trickle of money coming in, although not much compared to the vast outlay, time and trouble taken to renovate the place.

By contrast, the house next door to this non-seller went instantly for £600,000, in its raw state. The house had all the horrors that make the TV presenters shudder – a tarpaulin-shrouded motorbike in the front garden, a tasteless front door, disgusting kitchen, avocado bathroom. Nobody had 'staged' this house, nobody had 'presented' it and yet it sold the minute it went on the market.

Why? Simply because buyers who are interested in this type of house in this price bracket can see straight through the cynical 'done up to sell' look and they largely prefer to do places up them-selves, in their own time and in their own way. They are, in the main, people who do not want a developer's perhaps bad taste imposed on them. The renovated house had a cheap kitchen and laminate floors, whereas discerning buyers in this market want an expensive kitchen and real wood floors. They don't want to pay top dollar for a new kitchen and new flooring that they can't live with.

There have now been so very many television property makeover shows that ever more people can see through the 'done up to sell' look. Journalist Catherine Ostler wrote in the *Evening Standard* magazine, 'Having spent almost a year selling my flat... I can recognize all the desperate seller's tricks immediately... . If the occupants are under 40, they will have wooden floors, magnolia walls, Arne Jacobsen dining chairs and children's names on the door in painted letters. The house will have been "knocked through" to within an inch of its life, and the side return will have been "done", conservatory-style.'

The trouble is, the builders who developed the non-selling house didn't take into account that potential buyers for this type of property, in sophisticated West London, would be members of the chattering classes who read all the books, watch all the programmes, gossip among themselves and generally remain one step ahead of the game.

Other points to bear in mind

Where did these developers go wrong? Mainly, they did not research their market closely enough. They did not have in mind an identikit buyer, which you must do, whether developing, buying to rent or doing up to sell. You must establish what this person looks like by doing rigorous homework, looking at similar properties and discovering which features sell or do not sell a home to this person.

The house that did not sell is not an isolated example. I have come across many instances where clever-dicks buy dilapidated houses, do them up according to what they imagine is the contemporary style, then find that they hang around, while grottier houses in the same area go for almost as much.

Catherine Ostler also made the point that hardly any houses she viewed had books. I've noticed this, too, and yet I personally would not want to buy a property from somebody who didn't read, as they wouldn't be on my wavelength. They wouldn't have made provision for bookshelves. I have over 3,000 books in my house, so, if I sold, it would likely appeal to another booklover. Ann Maurice, the television 'House Doctor', believes that more than a few carefully placed books constitute clutter, but for booklovers they are essential décor. Sorry, Ann, but in my world books do furnish a room.

The same is true for other interests, too. Someone who loves to cook would not buy a home that had a minimal kitchen without a good-sized cooker and lots of storage and worktops. Couples with young children will not go for houses that are not child-friendly – with balconies, no bath, lots of stairs and a deep pond, for example.

It is not only essential to discover the state of the market and the type of buyers interested in your area before spending any money on improvements, but also to have *empathy* with the target market. You must not only know, but intimately understand, the market potentially interested in your property. Do up a place without bookshelves in an area that attracts mainly media types at your peril.

Yet, if developing in a downmarket area, you have to go with that taste, as well. When I worked on mass-market newspapers and magazines, we often carried reader offers. The worse the taste of the offer, the more popular it was! Anything plain and in good taste was never snapped up by our readers.

Swirly carpet is supposed to be the number one horror. Yet, when I visited a friend recently, she said, 'I like swirly carpet! It lasts longer than plain, doesn't show the dirt and can warm up areas such as stairs and landings. Plain carpet soon looks filthy and you can never satisfactorily clean it.' So, in order to go with the prevailing taste, you may have to forget your own standards and apply those of your target market.

The state of the market in any one area can be ascertained by looking obsessively in estate agents' windows and, if you are cheeky enough, going in and asking them what sells, for how much and why. Then, if you have the brass neck, you should arrange to view some properties to see what you get for your money in your chosen area. This is what Nicola Naish did:

Before buying our first property to renovate, I spent ages viewing one-bedroom properties in the area we identified as up-and-coming.

I wanted to be comfortable with what we were doing, and didn't want to get out of my depth, which is why I concentrated on one-bed flats. From looking round, I realized that the gap in the market was for smart one-bedders in central locations. There was more or less nothing like that on the market already.

Then I started to look for signs of regeneration. I hit on the area when I discovered that, over the past three years, upmarket restaurants, kitchen shops, designer shops and an upmarket hotel had come into the location. I needed to know that I could add real value to the target market, so the next step was to identify this market.

It seemed that the greatest need was for contemporary one-bed flats aimed at people who were not real homemakers and who would not be spending much time in the property, but wanted a smart place to impress their friends. This market would not be interested in a sea view, yet would want to be near the sea. Nor would this market want a garden.

So I started looking for large houses that could be divided into flats, but would not appeal to a family. We felt that if we renovated a five-bed house for a family in the centre of town, we would struggle to find buyers and probably end up not making a profit. The risk factor was too high. In the end, we did find an ideal property, but dealing with the council and meeting all the regulations was an absolute nightmare. We also had to know, before we bought, that we would actually be allowed to convert a property into five flats. The area we hit on has just been designated a conservation area, which meant we could not put in uPVC windows or doors, for instance.

We were looking for a location that had started to come up, but still had a long way to go. The market was for low-price single dwellings that at the same time were smart, easy to maintain, central and impressive. It's hard to make money unless you define your market as closely as this. The stakes are too high to take undue risks. You have to go on as many certainties as you can find.

I must admit that I am one of those dreaded 'phantom viewers' who look round properties with no intention of making an offer. Yes, I'm a time-waster, but I always kid myself that if I really like it, then maybe I will make an offer. Also, by continually looking, I am keeping my eye in and discovering what sells, what hangs around and what kinds of locations and interiors are most popular. I am also keeping abreast of those small shifts in the market that you ignore at your peril when trying to make money from property.

Don't forget that estate agents, above all others, are trained to be polite, courteous and helpful. You can also ask them whether extensively refurbished homes are snapped up more quickly than those needing a bit of work. It is important to know how long properties remain on the market before being sold. A website such as Hometrack will give this information for specific postcodes.

The property market is different in different parts of the country, too. In Milton Keynes, for instance, where house prices are going up at a terrific rate at the moment, there is always more demand than supply. A friend who works at the Open University was looking for a three-bedroom home in Milton Keynes. She said, 'Every time I saw a house in my price range and contacted the agents, it had gone. In the end, I just bought the first house that fitted my needs, knowing that it, too, would be gone in an instant if I didn't snap it up.'

In places such as Milton Keynes, where house prices are going up fast, it is relatively easy to add value. The thing to do in a place like this, full of modern estates, is to make your property stand out from the rest. A conservatory will add value, as will a landscaped garden, smart new carpet and stylish curtains. The less bespoke the house is in the first place, the easier it is to add some value by making yours a little bit different, a little bit more upmarket. Milton Keynes has a very mobile population, where people only stay in the same house for two years, on average, before moving on.

Because Milton Keynes is a thriving place, property values, even for the mass-produced housing, are going up fast. In fact, just about all the residential property in the area is mass-produced and the better presented it is, the faster it goes. My friend knows that she could sell her house tomorrow, at a considerable profit.

When considering buying something as expensive as a home, it is essential to discover what kind of market, if any, such a property appeals to and if, in general, properties in that area have gone up or down in the past year or so.

To take another example of how important it is to ascertain the state of the market, I own two flats in adjacent blocks on the south coast. The blocks, both former hotels, are in high Victorian style and right on the seafront. They have a lot of character and some of the flats have balconies. Yet, although the buildings look identical, market conditions mean that flats in one block go instantly, while flats in the other building don't sell at all.

Why is this? Simply because the flats in one block are small, either one-bedroom or studios, whereas most of the flats in the other block are huge, with two or three bedrooms and two bathrooms. The thing is that, in Worthing, where these buildings are situated, the market for flats consists of first-time buyers and young couples, divorced and separated people, retired people downsizing and second-homers. All these types want something cheap, easy and compact.

The large flats in the non-selling block are beautiful, but there is simply no market for them. They are too big for second or holiday homes, too expensive for first-time buyers or the newly single and not suitable for families, who mainly want modern houses with gardens. Also, in this area, a family can buy a three-bedroom house for less than the flats – and they don't have to pay service charges on top of their mortgages either.

The big flats were formerly owned by rather genteel people, many of whom had been there since the 1940s. By the time they came back on to the market in the 1990s, the properties were extremely run down and were snapped up cheaply by amateur investors and developers – people who did them up lavishly at great expense and then expected to sell them at a huge profit. This did not happen because the would-be developers had simply not sussed out the market before embarking on expensive and extensive renovation. Sadly, these now-modernized flats won't even rent out, as there is not a significant rental market for three-bed flats in this area, either. So, they are sitting there, unsold and unlet, as an eternal object lesson to the no-brainer school of property development.

If these 'developers' had turned their big flats into two separate units, they would have sold instantly. Then, though, they would have needed planning permission and have to abide by building regulations. The would-be get-rich-quick amateur developers could not be bothered with this.

Whenever considering developing property, it is a good idea to contact the local council beforehand, to discover their housing policy. Is the council encouraging provision of single units? Are new businesses coming to the area? Are there any newly desig-nated conservation areas, where development permission may not be granted? Are car parks, hotels, offices or other buildings about to go up nearby? The state of the property market is one thing; what the local council allows may be quite another.

You also have to take into account average levels of pay and lending ability in specific areas. In most provincial towns without much industry, average pay is extremely low, so the amount securable on a mortgage will be correspondingly low. Do not develop beyond what your target market can afford.

There are a few areas that are so very desirable and sought after that you can spend almost any amount and still make a profit, but they are few indeed. They are really confined to prime central London locations and upmarket second-home villages. In Belgravia and Notting Hill, for example, you could ask a hugely inflated price and most probably get it, because this is a niche market consisting of extremely rich people. Plus, there is a finite number of properties in these areas and unlikely to be more any time soon. Richmond-upon-Thames, where I lived for 15 years, is another hugely popular location, attracting celebrities of the likes of Mick Jagger, Jerry Hall, Richard Attenborough, Hayley Mills and Lady Annabel Goldsmith.

You always have to ask yourself whether your property, or one you are considering, is in an area where people actually want to live. Then, there are always micro-markets within the larger market. Some streets in Notting Hill, for instance, are more fashionable than others. In Brook Green, where I presently live, there is a 'golden triangle' of streets where properties attract premium prices. Buy just outside this triangle and you could be doomed. So, there are always markets-within-markets, fashionable sides of the street and less fashionable sides, as Lady Bracknell pointed out in *The Importance of Being Earnest.*

In some areas of the North-East, such as abandoned ex-mining villages, properties have virtually no selling price at all. They are only suitable for renting to the poorest members of our society and can therefore only be sold on to people slightly more wealthy than them looking for buy-to-let bargains. There is little point in spending money on renovation when you can't even give a place away.

A friend inherited her parents' home. It was an attractive farm-house, set in several acres of land. By the time her elderly parents died, the house was in bad condition and needed total renovation. Her dilemma was whether to spend money on modernizing it or try to sell it as it was. In the end, after taking advice, she left it as it was and, two years later, it had still not sold. Nor had she received any serious offers. Hardly anybody was even interested in viewing it, whatever its condition or price. It did not sell at auction, either.

The problem was that it was in completely the wrong location – a Nottinghamshire ex-mining village where nobody particularly wanted to be. It was too far from major towns to commute and there was nothing much for people to do in the village. The villagers themselves preferred small, modern, easy-to-maintain houses to unwieldy 150-year-old isolated farmhouses.

Property renovation is not always a good idea!

In some parts of Devon, houses also have very low selling prices because there is no industry, most people are on low levels of pay and there is little to attract newcomers to the area. Places that are in desirable holiday or second-home locations, though, are another matter.

You have to be sure which category your property falls into. Before embarking on any large-scale renovation, I would spend a few months getting to know the state of the market in that particular area intimately; one trip round the agents is not enough.

Even if you are developing your own home rather than looking for a quick profit, you don't want to pour money down the drain – not least because circumstances may change and you may have to sell quicker than expected.

Another example: I once sold a beautiful Queen Anne house needing quite a lot of work to a couple whose dream home it was. They paid over the odds because they wanted it so much; in fact, they begged me to sell it to them. The husband was earning huge sums in advertising and they set about extensive renovation, believing that they would be there forever.

A few years later, the husband lost his lucrative job and could not get another. The couple had only just finished putting in a £100,000 kitchen when this happened and they were forced to sell. They made a good profit, but had not envisaged their circumstances changing so dramatically.

If your house is truly unique with nothing else you can compare it to, you can go to town more than if it is a mass-produced little box on a vast estate. Even here, again, you have to be sure that it is in a popular area. With a unique property, you may have to wait to ensnare the right buyer. Rich art dealers know that they may have to hang on to their paintings for several years before the right buyer comes along. When developing such a property, the same thing could well apply.

If you watch programmes such as *Property Ladder* and *Better Homes*, you will soon notice that, with few exceptions, hardly

anybody makes any real money from their property developments, whether this is their own home or a place that they have
acquired for investment purposes. This is not to say that there is
no money to be made in property development. There is. I have,
in my lifetime, sold many houses for a dramatic profit. My secret,
if I have one, is that I have always bought in areas of high desirability, where people are clamouring to be and so will pay over the
odds to be in that house or in that location.

It also helps to be a little bit psychic. Property developer Ivan
Twigden, who became one of the most successful businessmen in
the country, from a very lowly beginning, believes that one reason
for his success in property is that he sees things other people don't
see. In property development, this is vital. When interior designer
Jocasta Innes bought her Georgian house in Brick Lane for £7,000,
nobody much wanted to live in that part of the East End. Now, of
course, Brick Lane is ultra-trendy. Jocasta saw what other people
at the time did not see – that it was only a matter of time before
Brick Lane, with its central location, would come up in the world.
It is perhaps not altogether surprising that Jocasta's daughter,
Daisy Goodwin, is the producer responsible for most of the
property programmes on TV.

A famous spiritual law states that whatever you give attention
to manifests – to the exact percentage you give it attention.
Nowhere is this truer than in property development. All too many
people – professionals included – never give enough attention to
what they are doing and are then surprised when the desired
outcome does not happen.

Most property experts say that it is a serious mistake to pred-
icate your development on house prices rising. They may, but
they may also plummet – as they did in the late 1980s.

It is important to look for signs of gentrification in the area, but
don't forget that reverse gentrification can also happen, which will
also be your signal not to buy – at least if you're wanting to make a
profit. To give an example, if every Victorian terraced house in a
particular street has uPVC windows and doors, this means that the
houses have been modernized, but in the wrong way and it would
be difficult to overcome this. By contrast, if a row of similar
terraced houses have retained their original windows and doors,

the street has possibilities. Original features make an old property attractive and buyers looking for character emphatically do not want all the character to have been removed. Bolt-on uPVC conservatories, flimsy porches, satellite dishes, dirty windows, abandoned cars in the driveway, neglected front gardens – all are indications of areas to be avoided. Anything that is evidence of door-to-door 'home improvement' companies having successfully targeted an area also indicates a no-go location.

A recent report highlighted the top design crimes as being carpet in the kitchen or bathroom, dirty or paint-spattered light switches, dead or dying plants on show, overcrowded living rooms, gloomy interior lighting, limescale round the shower or bath, patterned or highly coloured carpets, stone cladding or pebbledashed walls and a badly built extension or porch. All of these 'crimes' reduce the value of a home, but the worst crime of all – knocking at least £10,000 off the price – is modern windows in a period property.

The Property Price Advice website

This is an enterprising – and free – method of working out exactly which features will add value to your property, and why. Property marketing expert Louisa Fletcher believes she has come up with the most precise method yet of assessing all the variables and coming up with an exact equation as regards adding value.

Although location works best every time, there may be major variations in properties with the same, or a similar, postcode. For instance, one place may be very near a noisy pub or main road, another may have a bigger garden and another may have off-road parking.

Louisa's system works on an algorithm, a method of evaluating individual properties by numbers and percentages. Every property, says Louisa, has a number of qualitative and quantitative characteristics that can be fed into the equation. For instance, an en suite can add 9 per cent to a property's value and an off-road parking space can add 6 per cent.

Louisa says: 'Most people rely on estate agents to value their properties, but these are never impartial as they may either overvalue a property to get the commission, or undervalue it because business is slow that week. They value properties according to what they believe they can get.'

Land Registry figures are also not completely accurate, according to Louisa, as they just tell you what a similar property in your area went for, and yours may be quite different. Yours may be in a better – or worse – location, have a sea view or balcony, be in a better position or be bigger or smaller.

Surveyor evaluations are also unreliable, she says, as these just look at the fabric of the property and not at any unusual features that may add or reduce value. 'Because we have no axe to grind, we can be completely impartial.'

In order to arrive at the valuations, Louisa takes data from the Land Registry, Office of the Deputy Prime Minister, local authority and financial markets. These give a base average value, by postcode, for different kinds of property. The method is complicated, but can tell homeowners whether it is worth their while adding a basement, loft extension, en suite or expensive kitchen.

The method can also determine the difference between marketability and adding value. A luxury kitchen may make a property more marketable but will not necessarily add value.

So what does add value?

Outside space, every time. An apartment with a balcony will always be worth more than an identical one without. We can statistically prove that original sash windows will add value to a period property, whereas uPVC windows will reduce appeal to buyers. A three-bed house with one bathroom will always be worth less than a three-bedder with two bathrooms.

Clearing clutter and painting walls in neutral colours will improve marketability but may not add value as it's space that does the trick every time. Extra bedrooms, bathrooms and parking spaces are always the major value-adders.

The financial benefits of additional bedrooms and bathrooms are quite significant, but if a house just needs cosmetic enhancement and a facelift but no structural work, the cost of this work would probably outweigh any increase to the property's value.

Houses that need cosmetic improvements are quite appealing to some buyers and, in my experience, properties of this kind often sell really well without too much improvement. There is definitely a market for properties that actually need some TLC.

So, to sum up, if you are adding significant space, you are most likely also adding significant value, but a 'tosh-up' will probably not make much difference to the value.

Here are some examples: a flat in Hampstead, North London, was valued at £435,000 and marketed as a one-bed flat. The owner discovered by logging on to the Property Price Advice website that, if he took out the shelves in his study and put in a bed instead, the flat could be marketed as a two-bedder, and its value would shoot up to £475,000 immediately.

A loft extension in a three-bedroom semi in Harrogate increased the value of a property by £70,000, making it worth £420,000 instead of its original valuation of £350,000.

Louisa concludes: 'You can usually add value by making improvements, but sometimes the cost of the improvement doesn't warrant it. There is not much point in spending £100,000 to add £100,000 to the place.'

The best thing, before embarking on any major improvements or renovations, is to check out the Property Price Advice website first, at www.propertypriceadvice.co.uk.

Is it a good investment?

If I am interested in buying a property in bad condition to develop, I always ask a builder friend to come and look at it, then give me a ballpark figure for total renovation, before I even think of making an offer. The unspoken quid-pro-quo is that my builder friend will get the work should I proceed with a purchase.

For the last two properties I viewed in this way, the figures just didn't add up. In both cases, I would have ended up spending far more money on the property than I could ever get back. This was because both houses already had a high asking price and, although improvements were much needed, even a modest makeover would have taken them way over any possible profit margin.

On the *Property Ladder* show, it's common for presenter Sarah Beeny to detail a tiny budget with which the developer hopes to renovate an entire house and sell it on for a massive profit. Then, surprise, surprise, the budget spirals hopelessly out of control, week after week.

On the more downmarket Carol Vorderman's *Better Homes*, which introduced a competitive element to the refurbishment genre, two families are invited to undertake major improvements to their own homes, after which estate agents come in and revalue the house. The couple whose renovation is considered to add most value wins a prize of £5,000.

Looking carefully at the sums in this show, you can see that the renovations add, on average, £4,000 to the value of the house – much less, probably, than the refurbishment actually costs. Also, any property valuation can only be inspired guesswork – you only know for sure whether or not you have increased its value when you have a firm buyer.

How do you know?

Good investments, as we all know, are those that you buy cheap and sell dear. With property, however, that equation is difficult to achieve, simply because property itself and all renovation is extremely expensive and the market is in a constant state of flux. There are also always, always, unseen costs. Houses or flats that are cheap are usually cheap for a very good reason: they are not worth more. Even when refurbished, they may not be worth much more.

If you are property developing, profit is all, so you have to do what you can to minimize the risks. On the *Property Ladder* show, we often see people undertaking their own renovations or calling in friends and relatives to reduce the costs, but this is a high-risk strategy in another way, as they might not be skilled tradespeople. Jobs badly done not only look terrible, but are spotted instantly by estate agents, who will immediately downvalue the house as a result.

When considering the investment potential, it's also important to work out how much the renovation will cost as a percentage of the house's maximum value. For instance, one of the properties I rejected had an asking price of £575,000. My builder told me that the renovation would cost at least £100,000 – and that was for the building work alone. It did not include painting, decorating, curtains or flooring. If I paid the asking price, by the time I had added on stamp duty, which people often conveniently forget (£23,000), legal fees (say, £1,000) interior decoration (£20,000 minimum), I would have spent £144,000 and there would have been no way, at the time, of selling that house for £700,000-plus. The ceiling in that street was around £630,000.

Experts estimate that, in order to profit from renovation, you should be able to show a 20 per cent clear profit. If I had spent a total of £644,000 on this development, I would have had to have sold it for £762,000 – an impossibility. I haven't even added on capital gains tax, which, with such a quick turnaround, would have come in at the full 40 per cent of the profit.

When considering a property purely for its investment value, you have to know where you can save and where you should spend. Central heating and up-to-date wiring systems are a must and they have to be done first. Smart kitchens and bathrooms are also essential and these cost a basic minimum. Cheap kitchens and bathrooms will cost as much to install as expensive bespoke appliances and suites. If you are dividing a property into flats, you will have to soundproof the units, which could mean putting in steel ceilings at vast expense.

Similarly, conservatories, extensions, loft rooms, extra bathrooms or showers are all expensive and may need planning permission before you start. If your alterations are so complicated that you have to employ an architect, you can add on even more.

When I bought my present house in 1994, I was interested in turning the side return into the type of conservatory sneered at by Catherine Ostler. I got in three quotes, averaging from £30,000 to £45,000. I had bought the house for £200,000, so these sums were too large and could not possibly be recouped on resale. Ten years later, I actually achieved the conservatory extension, at a cost of £25,000 – less than the original quotes of a decade ago. By now, though, not only was the house worth in excess of £600,000, but many other houses in the street had gone in for similar extensions.

So, even if my extension didn't actually add value, by not improving my property in this way, it would have lost value. It would have compared badly to the other, similar houses in the area. Sometimes, it is important to keep up to date just to protect your investment, never mind increasing its value.

I was once interested in buying a two-bed maisonette on a former council estate as an investment. The maisonette was in excellent condition, but its asking price was high – probably right at the top of what the market at that time would have accepted. The flat had an integral garage, which could easily have been converted into a third bedroom, thus vastly increasing the value and scope of the property.

I was quoted a ballpark figure of £5,000 for converting the garage into a bedroom. The only fly in the ointment was that of obtaining planning permission, so, before putting in an offer, I called the council. Their indications were that planning permission was unlikely to be granted as parking was already tight in the area and permission had previously been refused for similar applications.

I might have been given planning permission, but decided the risk was too high. With only two bedrooms, the market for this property would remain limited. As it turned out, the maisonette remained unsold for many months, in spite of its generally top-notch condition, for this very reason.

As a property obsessive, I have seen too many nicely refurbished properties in desirable areas sticking on the market not to be very, very careful indeed before I would purchase anything purely as an investment.

When buying purely for investment, it is also important to bear in mind that, sooner or later, your place will need a complete refit. Here is a personal example: in 1998, I bought a large studio flat for £33,000 and it was rented out at £350 a month – not a bad percentage return. At the time, it only needed minor decoration to make it habitable.

However, in 2006, it was no longer rentable as it was and had to be taken off the market for an expensive renovation job. This renovation cost £11,000 and the achievable rent was now £450 a month. The value of the property had gone up to £105,000 but of course the percentage rental yield was now much lower. However, I had no choice but to renovate as the place had become too dingy and old-fashioned to be successfully rented out as it was.

There was also, by now, no way of toshing up the place and it needed everything doing – new kitchen, new bathroom, new flooring, wiring, complete redecoration and furnishings.

There was also, at this point, no real way of recouping the cost of the renovation either on increased rent or on resale. But the renovation now in place will last for ever – or for at least 20 years. For the foreseeable future, it will only need minor redecoration between tenancies, and this illustrates the point that sometimes, when renovating, you have to forgo short-term gain for the long-term viable future of the property.

The other factor is that this particular flat is situated in a town that is fast coming up in value and desirability, and where incoming residents are looking for something smart.

Developing or renovating your own home

When considering improving your own environment, there are three main questions to ask yourself:

- Could I recoup the cost of the improvement on resale?
- Will the renovation I am thinking about enhance my lifestyle?
- Will the work I am thinking about actually add value?

When developing or improving your own home, there is clearly not the same need to keep a beady eye on profit margins as when buying purely for investment. Lifestyle considerations are equally, if not more, important. At the same time, as we have just seen, you do not want to carry out work that will decrease the value of the property in a buyer's or agent's estimation.

What helps and what hinders

Anything really quirky or unusual may limit the market and, remember, tastes change extremely quickly these days. Also, what looked good a decade or even five years ago will now look dated and may need changing. Yet your home is, or should be, a reflection of yourself, so you do not want to live with a completely bland, neutral interior on the off chance that you may want to sell it one day. The secret when renovating your own home is to make sure that any improvements are in keeping with the general age and style of the house. uPVC windows and laminate floors cheapen a Victorian house, but may be very suitable in a small modern flat.

In general terms, anything that makes the house seem bigger, lighter and more airy and modern – without losing its essential character – will add value or, at least, not take it away.

People these days appreciate eat-in kitchens, bedrooms that can take a double bed, en suite showers, where possible, and big living rooms. They are also looking for loads of storage, which UK homes, ancient or modern, very often don't have, at least when compared with US homes. Up-to-date electrical and heating systems, however old the house, a roof in good condition, pointing in good condition and attention paid to the outside, all keep up the value and desirability of a home.

If it is your main home, lifestyle must come before profit. Likewise, if it is a second or holiday home. Although you must do everything you can to not take away any value, don't forget that you are enjoying the value the whole time that you are living in a lovely home in a wonderful location. You cannot put a price on happy memories and an attractive environment. I did not buy my holiday home on the South Coast as an investment; if it goes up in value, that is a bonus, but nobody can take away the wonderful times I have enjoyed there looking at the ever-changing moods of the sea.

Where there is limited renovation money, as there usually is, you have to decide what is most worth doing. If I am moving to a tired old house, the first thing I tackle is the garden. I have done this in several homes, for the simple reason that gardens take time to establish themselves, whereas bricks and mortar improvements show results instantly. Also, garden work is dirty, especially if workers have to come through the house.

Then, I think the most useful improvements are those that will greatly enhance your day-to-day life. For some people, this may be a second bathroom. In any case, I would always try to put in a downstairs loo. So many older houses simply don't have them, but they are an absolute godsend. You can hardly have too many!

Never take away a bedroom if you can possibly help it. Most people would prefer an extra bedroom to an en suite bathroom and, in any case, the more bedrooms, the wider your market – that is, in a market where families congregate at least, as, in markets where money is tight, people may not want to pay extra for another bedroom they are never likely to use.

I live alone in a three-bedroom terraced house, but often have people to stay. Because of my frequent visitors, it would be lovely to have an attic conversion with en suite shower room. However, I decided on a kitchen extension instead, as I couldn't afford both, and I have not regretted it because I enjoy my now huge kitchen-diner every single day, whereas I would not use the loft extension myself – it would have been purely for my guests' benefit.

I also know from my research that those interested in buying in my street like to have an enormous kitchen that gives them wonderful entertaining space, but, because there is only a small patio garden, the house is not really suitable for young families. The target market is either older single women like myself, young high-earning dinkys, (double income, no kids yet) or gay men in partnerships; all of whom either have high salaries or, like me, are downsizing to a smaller house now the family has grown up or because of divorce.

A feature in *House Beautiful* magazine gave a list of home improvements that are worth the investment – and those that aren't:

▌ with a loft conversion, you may just get your money back;

▌ an extension on the ground floor will almost certainly add more value than the cost of the work;

▌ adding a downstairs toilet will give you back the cost and increase saleability, but may not add actual value;

▌ adding a porch is unlikely to add any value;

▌ a conservatory will only impress if it can be used all year round;

▌ installing a new kitchen will give you back what you spent;

▌ adding an en suite bathroom should give you your money back, at least;

▌ replacing windows with double-glazing is unlikely to add value and, if you put uPVC ones into a period property, this will take money away;

▌ turning two rooms into one is not usually an expensive item, but will most probably not get you back what you paid either.

Other pointers

Renovation experts and estate agents are increasingly saying: ditch the dining room! Dedicated dining rooms are rapidly becoming redundant and the smart money is now on making the kitchen as big as possible and doing away with the dining room altogether. This means the kitchen is coming ever more into its own.

Nowadays, families do homework, chat on the phone, do paperwork and entertain in the kitchen. The best thing to do with a dining room is to turn it into a home study – but make sure you designate it as such. The bigger the kitchen, the more value will be added.

The more light you can bring into your home, the greater its value. Nobody these days likes dark, dingy, small rooms. Open-plan is the thing, and wall-free interiors are increasingly prized.

Another unusual way of adding value to your home, if it is an old property, is to trace its history, especially if its use has changed over the years. Henry Holland-Hibbert of Lane Fox says: 'People who come to view an old house love a bit of history and any local stories or old photographs add interest and value. The sense of history helps new owners feel a connection to their home.' This is the case even if there are dark secrets attached to the home, such as somebody being murdered there centuries ago. So – check out whether your property has any interesting history attached to it.

Personal example: I have a flat in a high Victorian building that was once five separate houses, and then became a hotel before being turned into flats in the 1940s. The building also housed many soldiers coming back from the Second World War, in bedsitters, which were a new idea back then.

This information is always interesting to potential buyers of flats in the building, and should, in my view, be included in any seller's pack.

Now for the nightmares…

When renovating, these are the things *not* to do; they are sure-fire value losers, according to TV interior designers Colin McAllister and Justin Ryan:

1   Big 1980s-style veneered, laminated units with frosted glass doors, a video shelf and built-in aquarium are the most offensive items in home decoration. Some people dedicate up to 30 per cent of the floor space in their living rooms to these disgusting items.

2   Collections. Lots of ceramic doll's houses, swords, ornaments, plates mounted on the wall, hundreds of family photos and suchlike must be got rid of in any home of taste. They are relatively easy to dispose of but can lose your home as much value as plastic front doors and double-glazing.

3   Net curtains on cafe-style tension wire. According to Justin and Colin, net curtains are reminiscent of Les Dawson sketches with two heavyweight housewives talking over the garden fence, wife-swapping and swinging parties.

4   Shell-backed sofas. Nuf said.

5   Heavily patterned carpets. Here is a true story: a neighbour of mine recently bought a very large flat that had been on the market for more than two years without a whiff of interest from buyers. The reason? It was entirely covered in the nastiest patterned carpet anybody had ever seen. All my neighbour had to do was pull it up – yet this simple solution did not seem to have occurred to viewers.

6   Outsize home entertainment systems. Huge televisions and hi-fi systems look terrible, especially in a small room.

All these are home dis-improvements, guaranteed to decrease the value of your property. Other tasteless home improvements include removing wooden windows from period properties and installing uPVC ones. This can knock 5 per cent off the price, according to research carried out by Direct Line Insurance.

Other renovation crimes are: ripping out a fireplace or other period feature, concreting over the front garden to create off-road parking – this knocks about 2 per cent off the value – and putting a fish pond in the garden. Cheap laminate flooring is also a value-decreaser. The off-road parking space issue is not always simple, however, as parking is highly prized, especially in urban areas. Before concreting over your front garden, take advice from local agents as to whether this adds or decreases value, as preferences may depend on parking availability in an area.

In fact, any changes that are purely down to personal preference rather than aesthetically pleasing features will take value away from your home. So be careful that you are not spending large sums of money especially to decrease the value of your home.

Artificial gardens

No – this does not belong in the design nightmares section above. All estate agents and property experts talk about the importance of 'kerb appeal' whereby potential viewers will drive or walk past your place to see whether they want to go in. Dreadful gardens and dead window boxes are among the biggest turn-offs in existence, on a par with net curtains and shell-backed sofas. Yet it can be difficult to keep gardens looking good, especially if you have more than one home, are away a lot or are renting out a property.

The answer is to go artificial. Today's artificial plants and window boxes bear little relation to the dusty daffodils, wooden tulips and neon-coloured trailing ivy of yesteryear, and they can be the answer wherever watering is a problem, for whatever reason. It is a little-known secret that many of the lush, healthy-looking bay trees, window boxes and trees standing proudly in the multimillion-pound homes of Kensington, Chelsea and Belgravia are, in fact, artificial.

Roof terraces, basement patios, window boxes and even interiors can be made to look good with a few subtle artificial plants that don't die, don't need maintenance and provide welcoming, pretty greenery that can only enhance the bricks and mortar.

Writer Brigid Keenan, author of the bestselling book *Diplomatic Baggage* – a chronicle of her travels with her diplomat husband – found that artificial plants were the only solution for the roof terrace of her London flat. From reluctant beginnings, Brigid has become a total convert to artificial greenery in places or situations where real plants are liable to wilt or die.

Buying to let

Here, you really cannot afford to make mistakes or pay over the odds for renovation or redecoration. Every single penny has to count because with buy-to-let you are essentially establishing a business on which you will have to pay tax and make annual tax returns. At the same time, the buy-to-let market is becoming smarter, more sophisticated and competitive all the time, which means that a dingy, dated rental apartment will not appeal.

Some landlords like to buy places that need just a little bit of work as they believe that they will thereby get a bargain. However, that 'little bit of work' needs to be done before you can hope to rent the place out.

Briefly, these are the main questions to consider before embarking on buy-to-let:

▌ What is the actual rental market like in your area, both in terms of personnel and achievable rent?

▌ What is the supply?

▌ What is the demand?

As when buying a home, those who rent will only be able to afford to pay a proportion of their salary. There may be a slight premium achievable for a really nice flat in top-notch condition, but it will not be a significant extra. So you need to find out from letting agents which are the most popular types of rental property in any one area and how much tenants are prepared to pay or can afford to pay. Also, discover whether or not any particular area already has a huge glut of rental properties awaiting tenants. You may not feel you want to add to the oversupply.

Then you have to find out how much you will have to pay for your property, how much it will cost to do up and how much you can hope to achieve in rent. These figures have to be worked out very carefully indeed, with every last penny budgeted and accounted for. Unless your figures indicate that you can achieve at least 7 per cent of the total purchase price, including renovation, in rent, the property is best avoided as otherwise the margins are too narrow and would not allow anything spare for emergency repairs or renovation. You cannot operate too near to the margin as, above all, rental properties are bought in order to achieve instant or near instant income.

With rental properties, you cannot take the possible capital growth into account, although, having said that, there must be an achievable sale price. Beware of properties that seem suspiciously cheap.

A three-bedroom flat in a high-rise was recently advertised for sale in London W14 at the absurdly low price of £180,000. Flats this size would usually be offered for sale at £250,000 at least, especially in a desirable location just opposite a tube station, as this one was. Normally, you cannot buy even a small studio for this price in this area.

Intrigued, I went to have a look. The property needed some work – a new kitchen, new bathroom, new flooring and redecoration. This would have come in at £10,000 or maybe even less, which would still have made the flat a bargain, especially as the achievable rent would have been in the region of £350 a week. The yield, therefore, would have been over 9 per cent – mostly profit as service charges on this ex-local authority block were also very low even though the block was well-maintained with no graffiti or rubbish in the common areas.

A bargain, then? No. The downsides stacked up too badly. For one thing, the lease was less than 50 years, and not extendable, and, as the flat was on the fifteenth floor, no mortgage lender would advance money. This meant that the property would have no resale value at all. You would have to rent it out for ten years to get your money back and then you'd make nothing on it. So, there was no exit strategy. Its other major downside was that, while it had three large double bedrooms and a stupendous view, the living room was small and poky. Because of the arrangement of the rooms, there was no way that the living room and kitchen could be knocked into one, which would have maximized the space and thoroughly modernized the apartment.

I offered £50,000 for the property – about what I thought it was worth under the circumstances – but my offer was not even seriously considered. I would have gone up to £70,000 at a pinch, but, in the end, a cash buyer with more money than sense went for it.

Some personal facts and figures

I had a tough decision to make when wondering whether to rent out or sell my newly refurbished studio flat, referred to on page 30. The refit had cost £11,000 and, although I had not wanted to spend that much, there was simply no way of doing it any more cheaply as it had come to the end of its present habitable life.

In its original condition, the flat would have sold for possibly £85,000; in its newly renovated state, £105,000 maximum. I worked out that it would take around 15 years to recoup the cost of renovation in extra rent. But then, if I sold, I would have to pay capital gains tax as well as agents' and legal fees on the sale. I had spent more than 10 per cent of the value of the flat on renovation – twice as much as usually recommended. My accountant was all for selling – but in the end I decided to rent it out.

Why? As time went on, the spectre of capital gains tax, while not completely disappearing, would diminish. Both rents and property values might improve if I hung on to the flat, whereas if I came out with around £85,000 in cash there would not be much I could do with it. It is not enough money to invest with any hope of a decent return, and certainly not enough to buy another property.

Very often, the calculations involved when deciding whether to continue renting or to sell up, take the money and run do not give a clear cut advantage. For me, this was a choice of two not very good options, but what swung it for me was that the increased rent, although small, would yield around £5,000 a year, more than I would get on deposit at the bank and, with any luck, the value of the property would continue to increase. Plus – I still have the property.

Yes, there must always be an exit strategy, and you must know that your property is saleable, but it can pay to hang on to it.

There is also the point that any investment property will eventually require money spending on it. Even if it is not in bad condition at first, it will start to look dated after a few years. Renovation, whether for your own home or for an investment, is an ongoing process, not a one-off affair. Bricks and mortar require constant maintenance and, on occasion, this may mean a dip in your profits.

Raising the finance

Whether renovating your own home or developing for profit, the right finance has to be raised, somehow. There are various ways in which to do this. If you have a mortgage for your home, you can probably raise money quite easily by securing a home improvement loan or remortgaging. The vast majority of homeowners these days carry out improvements by raising money on the ever-increasing equity of their homes.

You have to make sure, though, that by so doing you do not extend the payback time indefinitely so that you end up never repaying the loan.

If you can pay cash, then you just pay cash and have done with it. This is obviously the ideal, but most of us are not that lucky.

When raising money for buy-to-let properties, second homes or development, then obviously interest rates have to be carefully taken into account as even a quarter of a per cent increase can throw out all your careful calculations. If you can pay cash, then you are in control, but if you need to raise finance, lenders will look very carefully at your situation and decide whether or not you are a good risk.

You can obtain special mortgages for self-build homes and the range of other loan possibilities is being extended all the time. Whichever loan package you go for, however, it has to be borne in mind that mortgages and loans are sums of money on which large amounts of interest have to be paid, over many years.

In my street, everybody but myself raised money for their improvements by remortgaging. As I bought my home for cash, I had no credit history – or at least no recent credit history – and could not borrow any money. So, I had to pay cash or else not have the improvements done. As with anything else in life, there are pros and cons to not having debts or mortgages, but at least I do not have the worry of having to pay back a loan. Lenders are remorseless – they never forget, whether you can pay back or not. As actor Richard Briers once remarked, 'People don't like you when you don't pay your bills.'

If you develop a property or purchase a buy-to-let with a mortgage, don't forget that the property can always be repossessed if you can't meet the loan repayments. The longer your property lingers unsold or unlet on the market, the more these payments will stack up, without anything coming in in the meantime. Also, you must have a specific buy-to-let mortgage for rental properties and this attracts a slightly higher interest rate than a mortgage for your own home. Strictly speaking, you are not allowed to rent out a property on an ordinary mortgage, although people do.

With buy-to-let, or when renting out a holiday home, you also have to remember that there is no guarantee that the place will always be occupied. Rental properties often experience void periods, during which the loan will still have to be repaid as usual. Capital gains tax will also have to be paid on the sale of any property other than your principal private residence and the government only allows each person or family one main residence.

It can be tricky to work out exact figures as there are many imponderables, but, whenever contemplating a property purchase, for whatever reason, take off the rose-tinted spectacles and look closely at the worst-case scenario *first*. Wishful thinking has no place in property improvement – the whole process is too complicated, too disruptive, too expensive and causes too much wear and tear on your nerves for shaky finances to be added to the mix.

Good renovations are extremely expensive and should never be undertaken unless you know for certain that you have all the money in place or can raise it.

More finance details

A word you often hear on television renovation programmes is 'contingency'. This refers to a sum privately set aside for unexpected costs, of which there will always be some. Often, it is not possible for builders, with the best will in the world, to quote accurately for a job until they start unpicking the fabric. So make sure there is always some contingency money available before you start. Or – wait until there is, to avoid sleepless nights.

It is safe to assume that your renovation will always cost more than quoted and that there will always be extras. If you do not have the cash in the bank, ask your bank or building society about a home improvement loan and take all the paperwork with you, before ever embarking on any major renovation. Home improvement loans are now firmly established as bona fide lending, but the lender will want to know that the improvement will definitely add value.

As with any loan, there will be interest to pay, and this is all part of the number-crunching you must do before getting started.

'Staging' the property

Whether you are renovating for profit, buying to let or selling your own home, do not forget the importance of 'staging' your home. This is a concept introduced to the UK by House Doctor Ann Maurice, with such success that buyers or renters now expect it.

Put simply, 'staging' means giving the buyer or renter an idea of the kind of lifestyle that would be lived in the home. This means putting up curtains or blinds that match the standard of the improvement, a few simple pieces of furniture to indicate that, yes, you can get a double bed in this room and, yes, you can seat four in the dining area in the kitchen and so on.

If the property is new or newly renovated, it should be warm, have fresh flowers and plants and a few ornaments, books and pictures and a sofa with attractive cushions. A few upmarket magazines (up to date) placed on the coffee table are also a good idea. Although professional designers and developers can see through this staging, the ordinary buyer is impressed by it, every time.

Nicola Naish is certain that her show flat went within an hour of being unveiled, for the full asking price, because she had taken care to not only stage the property but also landscape the garden. The first impression was so favourable that buyers snapped up all the properties.

Gardens

The importance of first impressions cannot be over-emphasized. White gravel will always look good in a small front garden. At the very least, make sure the front area is tidy and free of builder's rubble before you put the place on the market.

If you will not be there to look after a real garden or real flowers, consider artificial, as detailed on page 36. Lettings agent Claire Gibb, of the London agents Bective Leslie Marsh, said: 'We took on a property where the owners were in Argentina, and they asked us, the agents, to make sure we looked after the garden and watered the plants. But of course we can't do that, and so they all died.'

Do not embark on elaborate garden-landscaping if you are not going to be there to look after it as there is nothing worse than a neglected garden. At the very least, make sure the garden looks neat and tidy, and not as if you have to be Alan Titchmarsh to look after it. As lawns can be a pain, consider AstroTurf. Again, artificial grass has improved tremendously over the years and, when you are thinking about impressions, don't forget that an unmown lawn looks awful and gives the impression that the garden is an uphill struggle to maintain. Whenever you are not going to be around yourself to tend to plants, gardens and lawns, consider alternatives, such as paving, which will still create a good impression.

Conclusions

If it is your own home, lifestyle comes before profit, but make sure you do not embark on any renovation programme that will decrease the value of the property. You may like a sauna in the garden, a large pond or small swimming pool or Jacuzzi, but buyers may not. A friend put her lovingly restored house on the market, but one feature went against it: there was a fishpond in the garden. It was beautifully designed and had expensive koi carp swimming around in it, but to potential buyers it said, loudly and clearly: high maintenance. Not everybody likes fish or the fuss and bother of looking after them.

If it is a second home, ditto. Again, lifestyle comes before profit and, here, there is a little bonus to consider. As you will have to pay capital gains tax when you sell, you might as well spend money on the improvements you desire, which you may be able to set against tax, rather than give up to 40 per cent of your profit straight to the government when you sell.

If you are buying to let, the budget has to be worked out very carefully, and realistically, before you even make an offer on the place. Where every penny counts, you have to know where you can cut corners and where you can't. This is not the place for indulgence.

If you are property developing, you have to look for a place in an up-and-coming area and study the market very carefully. It is no use doing up a place so that it looks to be the work of a top designer and just hoping somebody will come and buy it when the market is simply not there.

Journalist Jasper Gerard, writing in *The Sunday Times* in December 2003, says:

> Only in Britain could it seem prudent to base an economy on the knocking out of pokey maisonettes after a half-cock Laurence Llewelyn-Bowen makeover... But it works, sort of. By convincing ourselves we will soon be bigger property magnates than van Hoogstraten, we borrow and we spend.

However, before borrowing and spending, a particular group of people has to be sought, engaged, cajoled, supervised and paid – the builders. We will consider these individuals in the next chapter.

2 Getting started

The general shortage of reliable builders does not mean that you have to grab at the first person you find. The golden rule when embarking on any property development or improvement is never, ever buy anything that needs substantial work *before* you know for sure that you can get hold of a good firm of builders to do the job.

One friend – who experienced problems with builders that were so horrendous lawyers are still involved several years later trying to sort out the mess – offers this advice, wisdom gained from bitter experience:

1. Never rely on friends to recommend you a specialist building service as what the builders did for your friends may be completely different from your project. Friends are so eager to help solve problems that they can forget the negative aspects of the people they are recommending. Sometimes friends can inadvertently do you a disservice.

2. Friends rarely warn you of the potential problems involved in a major project, such as the importance of having a properly qualified architect or designer before you start.

3. Before starting any expensive project, make sure that you have drawn up a proper contract with your builder and agreed an arbitration procedure if things go wrong.

4. Make sure that you look at the credentials of the people who have been subcontracted to do the work. Many of the 'qualifications' are worthless and merely refer to membership of an association that can be obtained by paying a yearly fee. Always choose people who belong to those trade associations that have a well-established grievance procedure.

5. Don't imagine that you are protected simply because you employ a well-known name. It is the person who is doing the job who counts, not his firm.

6 A dodgy builder knows a dodgy plumber, electrician, glazier and so on.

7 Keep a daily diary of events. If you don't you will wish that you had as, once the project is under way, so much happens so fast that it is impossible to remember all the details. You will then have a record of events.

8 Always remember that nobody is ever going to care as much about your building as you do, so always write down notes, however informal, of what you want done.

9 Never be bulldozed into quick decisions, otherwise you could end up with floor tiles you don't like, taps that are not what you would have chosen and cupboards placed in peculiar corners. Do not make decisions on the hoof, but always ask for time to think if you are not sure.

10 Deal with any problem immediately and never let it fester, as it can only get worse. If you wait to complain, the men could be off site, never to return.

If you are renovating your own home, then, of course, the work can usually wait until you do find the right builder. I waited ten years to have my kitchen extension done and it was worth the wait. Eventually, the right person came along at the right price and with the right know-how to do the job.

If, however, you are renovating or developing for profit, maybe you can't afford to wait. So, the best advice here is: never buy somewhere in dire need of massive amounts of work, only to find that nobody can do the necessary work for about a year. You will be throwing money away in the meantime. *Find the builders first, then buy.*

The builder–client relationship

Apart from the difficulty of finding a good firm to do work for you, there is the other factor – most renovation jobs involve developing an intimate relationship with your builders. We have seen on television programmes how very often developers and improvers sack their builders, only to find that they cannot replace them. Renovation magazines are full of stories of people starting out with high hopes, only to end up falling out with their builders and being unable to replace them.

In some ways, having the builders in is as intimate as a family relationship – even if it doesn't last as long. These people will be entering your property and will then proceed to not only destroy and demolish but also haemorrhage money out of your bank account at every turn. They need their stage payments as often as a blackmailer – and can hold you to ransom in as uncomfortable a way.

The right builders, tradesmen and professionals are integral to the success of any renovation work, whether it is undertaken for profit or to enhance your lifestyle. Where, though, do you find such paragons?

It's not easy, but, once you know what you are up against, at least you can ask the right questions to determine which contractor is heaven-sent for you.

How much do builders and other tradespeople charge?

Most of us only have building jobs done once in a while and so never build up great knowledge of what things cost. If you only have building work carried out every ten years on average, you may be shocked by how much prices and quotes have gone up in the interim. It is not unusual for plumbers these days to earn £50–£60,000 a year.

Most building firms tend to price jobs so as to give themselves around 15 per cent profit, which leaves 45 per cent for labour and 40 per cent for materials. Therefore, if you are providing your own materials, you can expect a quote to come in at 40 per cent cheaper than if materials are included. Make sure you are aware of which pricing policy is being used – does it include materials or is it just for labour?

It is becoming increasingly common to price jobs at so much a square metre or square yard, which makes it extremely difficult for ordinary, non-mathematical homeowners to work out what they will have to pay. At the time of writing, plasterers charge between £10 and £12 per square metre, plumbers around £130 a day (£60 an hour in London) painters and decorators, £80–£120 a day, depending on the area.

If your builder quotes you a figure per square metre or yard, ask for a price for the whole job. If you don't, prices quoted in this way always sound extremely small, then you get a nasty shock when the bill is for thousands of pounds. As you stand there arguing the toss, your builder can maintain that you agreed on £X a square metre or yard, which adds up to the figure now in front of you and you won't have a leg to stand on.

Be aware of the size and scope of the job

This is the first thing to ascertain. If the job seems unnaturally expensive, ask how the final cost is made up.

How much are the materials?

If a builder mysteriously quotes 'materials' as being particularly expensive, find out for yourself how much they really do cost before agreeing to the quote. Then offer to get them yourself. These days, anybody can get hold of building materials from suppliers – they no longer confine themselves to supplying the trade only, though they may be able to get discounts that you can't.

Builders' quotes usually come in two varieties: including or excluding materials. The latter type of quote, which is for labour only, seems much cheaper, but you will have to buy all of the materials yourself. My builder in London quotes for labour only, and I go with him to buy materials. My builder on the South Coast, by contrast, quotes for the entire job, including all materials and decorating. If you buy your own materials, at least you know you are not being ripped off. On the other hand, some builders use trade suppliers who are cheaper than the retail outlets. This saving may not, however, be passed on to you, the customer.

Sometimes builders exclude painting and decorating from their quote, and here you need to bear in mind that decorating is a highly labour-intensive job and can add several thousand pounds on to the price. Painting and decorating are also very time-consuming and it can take two weeks to decorate even a small flat, if done properly.

You also need to know whether your builder charges VAT, at 17.5 per cent, on top, as this will make the works much more expensive without giving you, the customer, the slightest bit of gain.

The VAT question is a tricky one, as most reputable builders will be registered for VAT, which is a government tax of no benefit to anybody except the government, including the builder. Sometimes builders will take cash but, against that, you do need proper receipts on headed paper and these may not be forthcoming with cash transactions that do not go through the books.

How much time will be needed?

Next, you need to know how long the job is likely to take. Get some ideas by reading relevant magazines, asking friends or neighbours, but never, ever embark on any expensive project until you understand its size and scope as accurately as possible. If it seems bigger and more complicated than you envisaged, it might be that your builder is trying to rip you off. For instance, I was once quoted £2,000 to replace a wall of tiles in a bathroom. I knew that the job, which involved replastering the wall, would take two to three days, but, as I was supplying the tiles, this seemed like extortion. Because I had received a written quote, I asked two other builders what they would charge for the same job and they both said £700. Don't forget, that this was for an *identical* job, not a cheaper version.

Should I get a quote?

The received wisdom is that you should get three written quotes (see Figures 2.1 and 2.2 for examples). In practice, this may be difficult as builders are notoriously allergic to writing anything down, so you may find it tricky to get even one quote. What I do in these circumstances is to read out the specification and ask another builder, over the phone, what he feels is reasonable for the job. If several builders give more or less the same price, then you can be sure that it is the standard amount for that particular job.

ANTHONY GREEN
GENERAL BUILDERS, KITCHENS, PLUMBING, BATHROOMS, PLASTERING & DECORATING

12 Brick Court   TEL/FAX: 01234 567891
Greater Rubble   MOBILE: 10987 654321
Hogginshire HS7 3YY

Mr and Mrs Kitchen
1 Up-and-coming Avenue
Greater Rubble
Hogginshire HS7 4££

28 April 2007

QUOTATION

To build up floor level to kitchen height.

To supply and fit softwood conservatory with French doors. Glazed, treated and painted.

To fit Saniflo WC in outhouse.

To remove and reroute plumbing in washing machine cupboard.

To relocate washing machine.

To extend worktop.

To have cupboard door made to match existing cupboards.

To supply and, if possible, match existing wooden kitchen flooring.

To brick up doorway in kitchen.

To raise manhole drain covers to floor height with inspection hatches.

Materials and labour £24,750

Figure 2.1 An example of a quote

GREG DAVEY

– ESTIMATE FOR WORKS CARRIED OUT AT:

2 LEAFY DRIVE

Kitchen and bathroom works

Remove all existing kitchen units and bathroom appliances and cart away.

Knock down wall and square off. Create new kitchen and bathroom wall.

Lower ceiling in bathroom.

Make good kitchen ceiling.

Fit new bath, toilet, basin and taps in bathroom.

Fit new kitchen units and appliances: units, new sink, taps, cooker, extractor hood, worktops. Rerun electricals where necessary.

Rerun pipework where necessary and fit to new central heating and hot water system.

Prepare kitchen and bathroom walls for redecoration.

Replace picture rail and skirting boards where necessary.

Price of works: £3,500

Already paid: £500

Date: 28.6.07

Figure 2.2   An example of an estimate

Most builders' estimates are very brief and lack detail. Architects' plans and estimates, by contrast, are incredibly complicated and abound in arcane technicalities. The reason for this? Architects are paid handsomely for their plans, whereas builders are only paid for their blood, sweat, toil and tears on site.

What should I do once I've chosen a builder?

When you decide to go with an estimate, it is a good idea to write a brief letter of acceptance, confirming all the details, such as that shown in Figure 2.3.

How bad will the disruption be?

You should also be aware of the level of disruption that the work is likely to cause and whether or not it might upset the neighbours. If so, warn them in advance and ask them to let you know if they are being unduly disturbed. Scaffolding, skips and Portaloos outside in the street for months on end will get on everybody's nerves, not to mention the noise levels from power drills and dust thrown up by demolition.

One friend was so badly affected by next door's building works that she suffered severe asthma and was in hospital for several weeks. She responded by suing the building firm for not taking proper anti-dust precautions and won substantial damages.

For such reasons and just as a matter of courtesy, it is always a good idea to consult your neighbours and at least inform them of what is going on well before works start. You may not need their permission, but you may welcome their cooperation – especially if things start to go wrong. Get neighbours on your side beforehand, show them your plans, introduce them to your builder and never take anything for granted.

2 Leafy Drive   1.7.07

Price Rising

Writecheques

Dear Greg

Thanks for your estimate, which we have pleasure in accepting.

Just to confirm our telephone conversation regarding works:

- you will start work on 7 July 2007 and hope to finish by the end of August latest;
- the price quoted is for labour and materials needed for rearrangement of the kitchen and bathroom; appliances to be provided by ourselves;
- the price quoted is fully inclusive;
- you will take full responsibility for the safety and security of the property during works;
- you will cart away all rubble and leave the site clean and tidy at all times;
- as this is a block of flats, you will be very careful not to disturb the neighbours, you will not work at unsocial hours and you will not leave any rubbish in the common areas.

We will pay you in regular instalments, on completion of works; the final instalment to be paid once works have been completed to our satisfaction.

All plumbing, electrical and plastering work is guaranteed for one year after completion.

We are very much looking forward to our new kitchen and bathroom, and also to working with you.

Best wishes

John and Liz

Figure 2.3   Example of a letter of acceptance of an estimate

Planning permission and other consents

When people apply for planning permission, they often feel that their local council regards it as their personal mission to block any alteration to house design and usage.

Be that as it may, any relevant permissions must be obtained, at least in outline stage, long before works commence and certainly long before you buy anywhere to renovate. If interested in a property that needs large-scale renovation, it is a good idea to check with the council as to whether or not any formal consents are needed for the work. In general terms, anything that alters the appearance or use of a building, such as an extension or loft conversion, will need planning permission, whereas something like a conservatory at the back will probably only need to meet building regulations. Some outbuildings may count as extensions; others as a new build or change of use.

Rules and regulations are becoming stricter all the time and vary from one part of the country to another. In some areas, there are rigid restrictions on what is allowed, especially if this affects the landscape, the roofline, any amenities or somebody's view. However, one person's eyesore is another's wonderful new home, so you never know in advance how the council will react.

Conservation areas

In conservation areas, there are always greater restrictions on alterations than otherwise. Designating an area 'conservation' always puts up property values, but, at the same time, imposes restraints on alterations. Rules are not as strict as with listed buildings, but the designation means that definite attempts are made to preserve the architectural integrity of the area.

In any case, never leave anything to chance. If you are not sure whether or not planning permission is required, building regulations apply or what you are planning comes under the guise of 'permitted development', it is worth making a call to the council involved early on to get an immediate reaction.

A glass roof, for instance, has to be made of special glass that is strong enough to walk on. New sash windows have to be double-glazed, which can cause problems when they need to fit into narrow Victorian window frames. You may have to abide by certain energy-saving restraints or ensure that insulation meets current requirements. You may have to use a certain type of brick or go for a certain method of construction.

Think of your neighbours

Whenever consent is required, plans must be submitted to the council many weeks in advance. It takes, on average, eight weeks to get planning permission – and that's when it's approved and goes through on the nod. If neighbours object, it could take even longer. When a planning application is received, notification is sent round to neighbours and notices are also posted on lampposts. Neighbours are then allowed to go to the council offices to inspect the plans and may object. However, any objection must be made in writing for you, the applicant, to view.

The key point here is to avoid disputes with your neighbours. If you have a problem with them, they could object out of spite and either delay or even cause the refusal of your application.

Then, of course, permission might be refused by the council. Do not ever assume that planning permission is always granted. However, it is reasonably safe to assume that if all other houses in the street have loft rooms, for instance, then permission for yours will be a formality

Listed buildings

Listed building consent is another matter and this must *never* be assumed. If you buy a listed building, you have to restore it in a way that is in keeping with the existing property, so you would not be allowed to replace wooden sash windows with uPVC ones, for instance. You would also need permission to knock down internal walls or alter the existing room arrangements, such as putting in a new bathroom or kitchen.

You will also need consent in listed buildings for certain other kinds of changes. This is necessary if, for instance, you are planning to turn two flats into one or one flat into two or considering turning the basement into a separate entity in a listed building. I once bought a house that had a listed wisteria. Heaven knows how the council would have enforced that one if we had cut it down.

The 'listing' process is a means of protecting buildings of historical interest. Listings were started in 1953 and are supervised by English Heritage. There are currently around 450,000 listed buildings in the country, and details are available at local authority offices. Listed buildings are divided into Grade I (usually very grand mansions), Grade II* (slightly less grand buildings) and Grade II – all the rest. Listed buildings are not always old; some 1970s buildings have now gained a Grade II listing.

If you want to alter a listed building, you need ordinary planning permission plus listed building permission. You can also apply for retrospective permission, but this is a high-risk strategy emphatically not advised as you can be ordered to tear down your alterations and replace them with the original. This order is subject to strict enforcement, and failure to do so can land you up with a large fine or prison sentence. Even if the works were carried out by a previous owner, you can be prosecuted.

It is usually much more expensive to carry out works to listed buildings, as very often windows have to be specially made, cornices may have to be specially ordered, and any external decoration or alteration has to be approved first. The idea behind a listing is to try to preserve, wherever possible, the original integrity of the building so that it remains a lasting monument to the architecture of its time. Therefore, you may not be allowed to erect ornamental gates or put up security gates or other security devices and you would certainly not be allowed to erect a satellite dish. If the building is in a terrace, a uniform look must be preserved. You can also be ordered to paint the exterior in a designated colour. For instance, all buildings on the seafront in Worthing must be white or cream.

It can cost 30–50 per cent more to renovate a listed building than an unlisted one.

If you are considering carrying out work on a rundown or historic property, you may be eligible for a grant. It is worth checking this out with your local authority before starting work. Not all authorities have the requisite funding, and grants are by no means guaranteed, but if a building is considered to be in a state of disrepair you may be eligible for financial help.

For buildings of true historical interest, historic property grants may be available from English Heritage. These are limited to very important buildings in need of urgent repair. Further information on this is available at www.english-heritage.org.uk.

Change of use

You will also need formal permission if you are thinking of changing the use of a building, such as turning an old barn into a home, an outbuilding at the bottom of your garden into a self-contained flat, creating a granny annexe or even building a porch or carport.

Also, if you are contemplating making a self-contained flat out of any part of your property, be warned: it will then constitute a separate dwelling and may be liable for its own council tax banding. Equally, if you turn a two-bedroom flat into a three-bedroom one, you may need to pay a higher band of council tax. I was myself (unknowingly) caught by the council tax trap when I turned a spare room into a self-contained flat and rented it out. How did I find out that I needed to pay? The Post Office had no record of it being a separate address and informed the council tax office. I then received a bill for several years' unpaid council tax.

Party wall agreement

If you are planning large-scale alterations to a terraced house, you will need a party wall agreement. This is a must – not an optional extra – as, when you come to sell, your buyer's lawyer will insist on seeing it. Such agreements are drawn up by specialist party wall surveyors who make detailed plans and take photographs of the existing arrangements to make sure that no agreement is infringed.

Some good advice

It is a good idea to talk to your local council planning department long before you start on any alterations. Also, don't imagine that these officials will be happy with a vague drawing scrawled on the back of an envelope. In any situation where regulations apply they will need proper architect's drawings.

If you are using a company that specializes in extensions and provides a complete package, they will arrange all this for you. Your builder should also always know whether or not any planned alteration needs formal consent. Avoid any builder who is vague on this matter as you are the one who will pay in the end.

A case in point: a friend bought a flat in a listed building where the windows were in terrible condition. She had them all taken out and replaced with uPVC. One day, a council official who happened to be passing by saw them, lodged an official complaint and the result was that my friend had to replace all the uPVC windows with wooden sash windows, at vast expense. She appealed, but nothing could be done.

You are not even allowed to put a satellite dish or television aerial on the walls of a listed building, so, if you are thinking of buying such a property, do not take anything for granted. Take advice first instead.

Bear in mind that, whenever you are planning alterations or improvements, officialdom is likely to come down on you with more and heavier bricks than the ones the builders will pull down. Don't be caught on the hop.

Buying a property to renovate or improve

Here, whatever you do, never take an estate agent's word that a place on the market you may be interested in buying needs 'cosmetic work only'. They will minimize the cost and extent of renovation in order to sell the place. It is only when the property is utterly beyond habitation that they will say the place needs 'total renovation'.

Also, never take their word for it that a place can 'easily' be enlarged or extended. I was attracted to the two-bedroom maisonette mentioned earlier because the agent's blurb indicated that planning permission to turn the garage into a third bedroom would be 'easy' to obtain. By calling the council, I established that such permission was unlikely to be granted. Other less cynical buyers might have imagined from the details that planning permission had already been granted, as that is what potential buyers were led to believe. However, I know from bitter experience that planning permission is never a foregone conclusion and you buy something without it at your peril.

Getting expert advice

If interested in a property that has seen better days, you can either have a survey done or call in a builder friend to give it the once-over. My own view of surveys is that they are largely a waste of money. Yes, I know they are advised in all other property books, so why don't I recommend them?

Because the surveyor wishes to earn his £150-plus an hour, he will prepare a long report detailing all the property's many defects. However, this does not necessarily give you an idea of what it might cost to put the problem right or if some problems can be safely ignored while others need urgent attention.

When, once, a party wall survey had to be carried out on my property, I was amazed to find every crack and wonky wall carefully detailed on the report. My house appeared to be in imminent danger of falling down, which wasn't the case, but, as the surveyor had charged my neighbours several thousand pounds for this report, it was going to be thorough.

Another neighbour paid a lot of money for a full structural survey when she moved into her house. The survey did not uncover the fact that the house was suffering from subsidence so severe that she had to move out for two years while the house was gutted and underpinned, then put back together at a cost of £150,000. It was two years before work even started as the insurance company argued that the surveyor had given the house a good bill of health and, therefore, it was a case of *caveat emptor.* Eventually the ombudsman had to adjudicate and he found in favour of the buyer, but it was touch and go. In the meantime, the house was valued at zero – and this was a half-million pound property.

A far better idea, to my mind, is to call in a builder friend, if you have one, or maybe a friend who has carried out renovations recently, to have a look at the property before you buy or even make an offer. In any case, I would get a rough estimate of the price of any job you are likely to undertake, then discover whether or not the improvements you are planning will actually add value.

Check how much work is required

If you decide to go ahead with your purchase, the next thing to decide is whether the job can be done by a handyman or needs a full team of architect, project manager, designer, engineer and array of skilled tradesmen, all of whom rack up the cost alarmingly.

Another factor to consider is your timescale. Bear in mind that the fewer workers you employ, the longer the job is likely to take.

There is also the question of how much, if any, of the work you are prepared to undertake yourself, remembering that, for any successful renovation project, you have to throw either time or money at the task – preferably both. If there is one point all the makeover programmes and their accompanying tie-in books agree on, it is that there is nothing worse or more offputting than unfinished, amateur or botched DIY jobs. Unless you know for sure that you can do the job as well as a skilled tradesman, it is better left to the experts – people who are doing it day in and day out – it could save you money in the long run.

When can work start?

Once you have bought a property, make sure that it is fully yours before you start knocking down walls. Years ago, when I was more naïve about such things than now, I hired a building firm to make alterations to a house that I had just bought with my then husband. Well, we had exchanged contracts and the previous owners had moved out, but we had not quite completed.

I was at work when I received a call from the outraged owner, who relayed down the phone the fact that my builders had knocked down a wall. 'Call your men orf!' she ordered. When I told my work colleagues, they advised, 'Ring her back and tell her you've changed your mind and you don't want the house after all.' It was tempting, but the matter was sorted out amicably after she calmed down.

Sometimes, sellers will give consent for work to be started before completion, but you always need a solicitor's letter to this effect and written agreement from the seller. You will at the same time also agree to become liable for utility bills before completion.

When buying to let, however, it is often a good idea to seek permission to undertake essential works before completion of the purchase, especially if the property is already empty. Every minute and every penny counts when you are trying to make money.

Paying for it all

If in theory the project is feasible, the next thing is to decide how you will raise the funds to do it. Very few people have the entire cash sum for a complete renovation sitting in the bank, but you will need to know that, somehow, you can pay for the works in other ways.

It is very dangerous indeed – complete madness, in fact – to embark on a renovation, especially one where costs can easily spiral, without knowing for sure that you will be able to pay for it. Many clients never pay the last tranche of the builder's money because they have run out of cash themselves.

Learn from the mistakes of the amateur developers on television, who appear to have an arbitrary 'budget' without costing the whole thing out carefully first. It is never made clear on the programmes how they manage to raise the extra money when they inevitably go way over budget, but that way lie sleepless nights at the very least and nasty lawsuits at the worst.

Getting quotes

Once you have a rough idea of the likely cost and extent of the job, you can then start getting in proper estimates – or quotes. Strictly speaking, an estimate is a guesstimate, whereas a quote is a firm price. In practice, though, a quote is rarely as fixed as it seems as, often, unexpected problems crop up that take more money to put right than the original quote allowed for.

Once you have obtained quotes, don't assume that it stops there as there will almost always be decoration and furnishing costs on top. It is rare that flooring, for instance, is included in a quote for an extension, yet flooring is one of the most expensive aspects of any renovation.

When you do receive quotes, read them through very carefully to see what is included and what is left out. Before booking up any builder, talk to them very specifically about which works are included and which are not. The quote should be very specific and include a rundown of costs.

Where do you find good builders?

Whichever method you use to find a building firm – whether by looking at work done in your area, recommendation from a friend or responding to an advertisement (dangerous, as busy builders simply have no need to advertise) – you must take note of the following before booking them up.

What does the firm seem like, generally?

If you are interested in using a firm that is already working locally, ask yourself:

▌ Do they arrive and leave on time?

▌ How do they leave the site each night?

▌ Do the builders seem generally in a good mood or are they always cross and stressed out?

▌ Do they clear away their rubbish?

▌ Is the skip emptied regularly?

▌ What kind of van do they have?

Ask to see recent similar work that they have done

If you are considering hiring a firm of builders unknown to you, always insist on this and ask to speak to satisfied clients. If the builders come with warm recommendations, then you will feel confident to proceed. All good builders will be only too pleased to show you their work.

A good tip is to wander in to properties in the process of renovation, apologize for being nosy and ask if you can have a look round. Mostly, I have found, the builders are only too pleased to oblige.

You can also ask the recent client if the job was started and finished on time and whether or not it came in on budget.

If you have a smallish job, a firm of builders working locally may well fit you in round a bigger job. There are times when they will be hanging around waiting for materials or tradespeople to turn up or may be stymied by bad weather. I have often called men in when working on another job to do some painting or decorating, for instance.

Do they send you a quote quickly and on proper headed paper?

This point is very important indeed – especially if you are hiring a firm previously unknown to you. Any reputable company will send a detailed quote, typed out (not in illiterate handwriting!) and, at the top, have a company name and a number for a land line. I am always suspicious of workmen who only have a mobile number and no headed paper – it doesn't look professional enough to me. The quote itself should be detailed, giving amounts charged for each aspect of the work. The quote should also indicate whether or not the job will need scaffolding, a skip, Portaloo or other equipment.

Should you negotiate on price?

Let's assume for the moment that you have contacted three firms of builders and received nice, detailed quotes from all of them. The only problem is, they contain wildly different prices for identical work. Quotes should all be around the same price, but often they are not.

When quotes vary markedly, I would always go for the cheapest – assuming that they are for exactly the same work. Very often, ridiculously high quotes are either trying it on or are deliberately pricing themselves out of a job.

Where the quotes are similar, as they should be, I would go, first, for the firm that can start soonest and, second, for those I liked the look of most.

In general, I would not advise negotiating on price, unless you are an expert yourself on building matters and know for a fact what the job should cost. Most builders will quote you a price that gives them 15–20 per cent profit and, if they want repeat business or would welcome your recommendation for new clients, they will want to be fair to you.

In my view, haggling gets the relationship (which is difficult enough as time goes on) off to a bad start. If the builders believe that they are being bargained down, they will often cut corners or show resentment in other ways. If the quote does come in at way above what you expected or were led to believe by your researches, leave that firm alone and try somebody else. I don't trust builders who overquote and then expect to be negotiated down. The whole thing then becomes a battle of wills and is the wrong way to go about the job.

Is your builder registered for VAT?

This is a tricky one, as, if they are, you will be quoted one price, then another with 17.5 per cent added on. Paying VAT is, from your point of view, money down the drain as it goes straight to the government and nobody benefits directly. For this reason, many clients ask if the VAT can be left off for payments in cash.

In situations where you have employed an architect or project manager, the price will always include VAT and you will have to pay it. Where the job is extremely extensive and you need to hire a firm that can cope with building regulations, planning permission, complicated rewiring and plumbing, then I believe you should go for a well-established company that charges VAT, as this is some mark of professionalism and that they have a healthy turnover.

If you are developing property or buying to let, then VAT will just have to be added on to the cost and there is no way of recovering it unless you have established a renovation business with a turnover of £50,000 or more. However, as buying to let is regarded as unearned income, rather than a proper business, you will not be able to reclaim VAT, whatever your turnover.

When paying in cash, note that you may not be able to prove the cost of improvements when negotiating capital gains tax on resale. For this, you need bills and you don't always receive bills when you pay cash. So, what you avoid paying initially, you may have to pay later. Don't forget that this government has pretty much closed all tax loopholes, especially those relating to property.

If you are renovating your own home, you may decide to pay cash and avoid VAT as capital gains tax does not apply here. However, whenever you do pay cash, make sure that you get a receipt for the amount, even if it is scribbled on the quote, as there will be no comeback later. I would never hand over large amounts of cash without getting at least some kind of written receipt, which must be signed at exactly the same moment as the cash is handed over, not a week or so later. You may be able to negotiate a slightly lower payment for cash, but your builder may be working on the black and insist on cash anyway.

I have to say that the last three builders I have employed in my home wanted cash payments, which they got. It kept them happy and also kept the VAT payments at bay. Building workers increasingly want cash in hand, to avoid paying tax. I am happy to help the black economy, but I must always protect myself first.

Is your builder insured?

I would say that this is a must for any but the smallest job and certainly essential if you are having works done that could constitute a danger to life. Wherever scaffolding goes up, there must be public liability insurance. Again, insurance adds to the cost, but I would never contemplate employing a builder who was not fully insured, except for the most minor jobs.

What kind of stage payments does your builder want?

Again, it is essential to check this out beforehand. Usually, builders ask for stage payments at the end of every month or when certain works have been completed. All this should be detailed on the quote. Do not give your builder any money up front, unless you agree to this as a condition of accepting the quote.

If your builder wants money for materials, before he starts, you can offer to go and get these yourself. Then, you will have receipts to keep and can be sure that you are not being overcharged. Alternatively, you can offer to go to the suppliers with your builder, so that you can pay for the stuff as it is bought.

It is also usual – at least for a major job – to retain about 5 per cent of the total cost until you are certain that there are no snags or problems developing. John Aylwin, a builder, advises:

> Don't release money up front, but offer to go with your builder to buy materials. Make sure you have arranged enough money to complete the job and insist on a retention for, say, three months.
>
> We usually accept 5 per cent as a retention. It is a good idea to lodge this retention money with a solicitor, otherwise the builder may believe that he will never get it. Problems so often occur over the last tranche of money, and if it comes to court, the client may say the builder did a bad job. Judges tend to believe builders are one step removed from thieves and will always believe the client over the builder, but, unless there is a retention, it may be difficult to get the builder back to finish the job.

The other thing to remember, says John Aylwin, is to make sure that you understand every stage and aspect, including payments, before hiring a firm. 'A lot of emotion is always tied up with a building project and, in any case, it is always going to be a huge financial exercise.'

Tip: Do not, whatever else you do, try to be clever and underpay the builder, or eke out the stage payments long beyond the agreed time, if for no other reason than that builders often have sneaky little ways of getting their own back.

Here is a cautionary tale: a project manager hired a small firm of local builders to undertake a major renovation on a large house. The work on the very rundown property was going to cost around £300,000 and was complicated and time-consuming. Stage payments were agreed at the outset but, when it came to paying, the manager shaved amounts off. For instance, if he had agreed to pay the builders £30,000, instead he paid them £10,000 in the belief that by being lean and mean he would keep them eager and on the case.

The exact opposite happened. Frustrated and angered by the manager not sticking to his part of the agreement, the builders went on a go-slow and eventually left the site altogether and the job unfinished. It was not possible to persuade new builders to come in at this stage, and the original ones refused to come in at all until they had been paid as agreed.

The result of this ploy was that the works took more than twice as long as originally estimated, and the new owners were forced to rent a property nearby from January to September, until the works were completed.

Many customers never pay the last stage of the money and, although this may sound smart in the short term, it means you can never get those same builders back to correct any snags, or to carry out a new job.

When can they start and when do they expect to finish?

Both of you need to be as exact as possible on this. Although start and finish dates must be flexible to some extent, you cannot be left in the air forever.

Will he be supplying drawings (if needed) and be responsible for obtaining relevant permissions from the council?

Any reputable building firm used to doing big jobs will be more than used to handling this kind of work. Your quote should state that the works are subject to the necessary planning consents and that, if approved, the contractors will put in train whatever official notices are required. They should never start any job until all consents have been obtained. It sometimes happens that 'retrospective' planning permission is requested once works have started, but this is a high-risk strategy, not to be recommended.

Conclusion

If you answer all these points long before contractors are hired, then you should not have any problems. However, when the worst happens and, in spite of all your careful research, your builders turn out to be from hell, what can you do?

The only thing is to cut your losses and move on. If your builder is from an established company, it may be worth going for legal redress. In practice, it may just happen that your builder disappears, never to be found again. In my experience, this can most often happen when the builder gives no land line telephone number or address, but just works from a mobile phone. If members of the various trades have a grievance procedure, then you can invoke this and may get compensation.

Whatever you do, however, try to keep your temper. Remain calm, and tell your builders that the relationship is not working out. However, I would always try to get other builders lined up before sacking the original ones. If you are becoming increasingly unhappy, source out another firm before sacking the original one and tell them the situation – builders often do not much like putting right the mistakes of a previous firm.

Are you builder-phobic?

If the thought of having builders in your house, ripping up your home and creating mess, disturbance and rubble for months on end brings on a migraine, avoid having anything to do with them where possible. Property renovation and development is only suitable for those who have the heart for it and who positively enjoy looking through kitchen and bathroom catalogues, going to showrooms, costing and planning the whole enterprise and looking forward to the finished result. If, instead, the prospect fills you with panic and dread, then avoid the whole thing. Property development is emphatically only for those who get a real buzz out of it as, even for the most enthusiastic renovator, having builders in can be stressful and traumatic.

Two friends of mine knew that their bathrooms badly needed replacing, but simply could not face the upheaval of doing so. They decided to live with them, dingy and dated though they were.

A lot of home renovation is to do with fashion, status and impressing your friends and neighbours. If, however, the whole thing fills you with horror, take a tip from Quentin Crisp and, instead of keeping up with the Joneses, drag them down to your level instead.

3 The professionals

As renovation jobs become ever bigger and more complicated, a whole raft of separate skills, trades and professions may need to be called on before your project is completed. Depending on the scope and extent of the job, you may decide to employ an architect, project manager, interior designer, landscape gardener and specialist kitchen and bathroom designer to ensure that you get exactly what you want.

Then you may decide to hand the whole thing over to the team of experts you have gathered together or you may want to have regular input yourself.

Let us look at what the professionals you may consider using for your project could do for you.

An architect

If your renovation or other plans are extremely complicated and need planning permission, or at least very careful drawings, you may consider employing an architect. Many people new to renovation are nervous of architects, having in mind somebody like Sir Richard Rogers or maybe a present-day version of Le Corbusier, who will cost as much as buying an original Damien Hirst.

However, architects come in all varieties and more and more of them are specializing in domestic conversions. The advantages of employing an architect are that you get professional-looking drawings and plans, there is usually a more interesting or exciting design element than a day-to-day builder could envisage and you also get somebody to oversee the works.

How much do they charge?

Architects charge between 10 and 20 per cent of the total costs, but don't imagine that they will be cheap. Two London renovations featured in the *Evening Standard* came in at £57,000 and £255,000 respectively – a far cry from the £10,000 or lower budgets featured on the average television property programme.

Architect Peter Thomas de Cruz specializes in dealing with domestic clients wanting to renovate houses – people who have most probably not used an architect before. His first meeting with new clients usually lasts for about an hour and he explains what he does, finds out what the clients want and talks about design. He feels that there is great scope for improvement in communications between architects and domestic clients.

Thomas de Cruz specializes in 'small' jobs, such as loft conversions, back garden extensions and interior remodelling. He charges around £3,000 for preparing designs for a garden extension, then clients decide whether or not to keep him on for project managing or oversee the works themselves. His internet-based work offers services in segments, so that clients can control their budgets. In fact, more architects than ever are offering informative services via the internet, so that potential clients can see what is on offer and get an idea of prices and designs before making a commitment to a particular architect who may not resonate with them (for more information, log on to www.architectsearch.co.uk).

Marion and Renske's experience

Marion Mathews and Renske Mann bought a holiday cottage in Devon in 2003 on a whim – a very expensive whim as it turned out, as the cottage, even in terrible condition, cost over £200,000. Total renovation would cost another £100,000 at least. In fact, the highly elaborate quote, running to seven pages, came to £96,563.08, including VAT. Four months after work started, it had already gone over budget, but they felt confident as the cottage, with a wonderful sea view, was in a highly desirable holiday spot where homes were already very pricey.

Marion says:

We felt we needed an architect as the renovations were going to be extremely complicated. Before we bought the place, we were told about an environmentally friendly local architect who would redesign the cottage sympathetically and also give an idea of the cost. We got in touch with him and he helped us negotiate on the price of the house.

We spent £4,000 on designs and a structural engineer before we even started. When the plans were submitted, the council didn't want to give permission for the new windows that were in the original spec, but our architect dug his heels in and they capitulated.

Because they were doing everything through the architect, Marion and Renske decided to get in only one quote: 'As we already knew what the work would involve and about how much it would cost, there was not a lot of point in trying to get more quotes. We are using local builders and I think that's important, as they have a reputation to maintain, and don't want to be accused of shoddy work.'

Years before, they had used an architect for another renovation and so were already comfortable with this kind of working relationship. They also felt that having an architect this time would put the whole thing on a more professional basis, especially as the renovation was very complicated. Marion adds:

Our view was that a professional was probably in a better position than two middle-aged women, especially when dealing with builders... Many women find that they have an uneasy relationship with builders, but an architect speaks their language and is used to dealing with them. Also, the architect is used to dealing with planning people and, because our house is 200 years old, we needed to know that the right materials were being used. When we bought the house, it had horrible uPVC windows at the back, but we are using traditional materials, as far as possible.

We are now dealing with the builders at one remove and, as we are a four-hour drive away from the cottage and working during the week, we can't be there all the time anyway.

Using an architect, Marion emphasizes, does not mean that you can leave everything to him:

> You still have to be hands-on and make sure you direct the architect. The architect, for instance, won't put forward suggestions; these have to come from you. What the architect will do, however, is to supervise the builders and make sure everything is done on time and to the previously agreed budget. The other thing our architect did was to draw up an electrical plan, so that the wiring could be put in place at an early stage. It's too late once you've plastered the walls.

More than ever before, electrical considerations are paramount as we have so much electrical equipment – there have to be enough sockets of the right kinds for computers, telephones, cable and satellite television, music systems and kitchen gadgets. You may need wiring for a bathroom. In my experience, bathrooms are almost always too cold in winter and need an instant wall heater in addition to radiators and heated towel rails. You may want to use an electric toothbrush. Think carefully about what you need or will need in the future as it will be too late once the plastering and tiling have been done. Architects think of things like this in advance, whereas people like you and me may not – it's their job, after all.

The look of the thing is important, of course, but practical considerations are paramount, as you are unlikely to be able to take it down and start again.

When and when not to hire an architect

When using an architect, you are definitely adding another layer of cost to the project, so this expense is probably justified only when renovating for your own purposes. Unless you are embarking on something major, such as turning a house into separate flats, using an architect for property development purposes would probably be too expensive.

Marion and Renske's house will have cost them over £300,000 by the time they have finished. They feel that they would not be able to make any profit on resale as that is the absolute ceiling price for that type of property in that area, but that is not why they are doing it. They are doing it for their own benefit rather than to make a big profit.

There is another consideration, too, which is that, as the Devon cottage is Marion and Renske's second home, they will become liable for capital gains tax when they do sell. The entire cost of the renovation can, however, be set against this tax.

Architects can often steer planning permission through where Joe public applicants might fail. They can argue for things in technical language and council officials listen. I have my own experience of this. The Queen Anne house I bought that I mentioned in Chapter 1 had been refused planning permission for two cars to park in front of the house, although there was plenty of room.

The council's argument was that, as the house was on an A road with double-yellow lines and right next to a bus stop, cars reversing out on to the main road would hold up the traffic. Instead, they had ordered the previous owner to put up a wrought-iron fence, to prevent cars from parking there. Yet, without the parking spaces, the house was virtually valueless as there was no other parking for miles around.

We took a deep breath and bought the house anyway (not a strategy I would advise for sensible people) and straight away set about getting the planning refusal overturned. We hired an architect specializing in heritage buildings, who was well respected by the local council. She drew up professional plans, argued our case and, eventually, was successful, thus doubling the value of the property overnight. There is no way that we could have had the decision reversed without the input of this particular architect. Twenty years later, the parking spaces are still in use, although in place of our old bangers are expensive sports cars.

To take another example, one couple bought a house with an integral garage and crossed their fingers that they would be able to get planning permission to turn the garage into a habitable room. Because they used an architect, permission was granted. In the main, though, councils do not like you turning garages into rooms as, if you do, everybody will want to do the same and this will create a parking nightmare.

Suitable architects specializing in domestic renovations can be found via their professional association, the RIBA.

One final point, it is very important to use an architect who is on your wavelength, will interpret your wishes sympathetically and stick to the budget you have in mind.

A landscape gardener

Increasingly, gardens are becoming a vital part of the general look of a property. When undertaking major renovation of a new home, I have always called the gardeners in first, before the building work has even started, and never regretted it. Gardens take time to grow and establish themselves.

The pros and cons

A landscape architect or designer can discuss suitable paving, planting and so on with you so that it fits in with the general scheme for the house. If you are developing for profit, it is enough to make the garden tidy, as landscape gardeners are expensive. Ten years ago, it cost me £3,000 to have my tiny back patio 'landscaped', but it was money well spent – you only need to have this extensive work done once. Marion Mathews and Renske Mann had the garden of their London home landscaped at an early stage of the renovation and it has given them pleasure ever since. In fact, I would always have the garden done, even if I could not afford any other improvements. If you think building work is difficult and dirty, garden work is even more so.

One important decision to make is whether to go for a high- or low-maintenance garden. Because I hate gardening, although I love gardens, I always go for the low-maintenance option. Your gardener can also advise on the right type of planting for your garden, taking into account whether it is north-facing, south-facing, the type of soil you've got and so on.

Gardens need to coordinate with the house, for that total look, so should be seen as part of the general improvement scheme.

A structural engineer

This professional may be required when the basic structure of a property is altered and when load-bearing walls are involved. Usually, architects will know of structural engineers or your builder will. In practice, the general public does not usually deal directly with structural engineers and they are only called in where the renovations and alterations are extremely complicated and call for mathematical precision.

Are they necessary?

Using their services will add another layer of cost to the project, so it has to be established that they are absolutely necessary to the success of the work you are carrying out. Structural engineers may be necessary with such projects as barn conversions, oast houses, windmills or any other renovation where a building not originally intended for human habitation is to become a home. They are not usually necessary for ordinary domestic renovation work.

A project manager

This is a relatively new profession and not one that comes with specific qualifications. In fact, 'project manager' is the smart new term for site foreman and denotes somebody who is responsible for supervising the workforce, ordering materials and making sure that everything is done in the right order and in the right way. Sometimes, a project manager may be an independent, autonomous individual, but is more likely to be the boss of the building firm you employ.

Do I need one?

All building works, even the smallest, need to be project-managed by somebody. In Marion and Renske's case, the head of the local building firm was doing the project managing, so, with the architect, they have two layers of overseers.

Unless you are very experienced in building work, I would not suggest project managing yourself, as this could constitute interfering in something you know little about. Before signing up any contractor, ask who will be doing the project managing.

In a building where I own a small flat, a decision was made to repair and renovate the entire exterior, at a cost of around £150,000. This was a complicated job that needed an external, objective project manager to approve each stage of the works. We, the residents, appointed a building contractor who was not involved in any of the works himself, but could report back and send us regular progress reports. For this work, the project manager received a percentage of the total cost of the work. It did not need an architect or structural engineer because it did not involve structural alterations, yet, because the building is listed, everything had to have the approval of the council. Our project manager arranged this as part of his job.

Project managers have to be aware of what is involved at every stage, so they must be people who know all about building and construction. That is why clients without such knowledge are ill advised to try to save money on complicated renovations by project managing themselves.

Keep on the case!

Although contractors do not like their customers poking and nosing about all the time, it is a bad mistake to go off site and leave them to it. More often than not, they will just go and do another job and you may find that nothing has been done for a fortnight. You should never hover around them permanently, but instead make surprise visits.

After all, it is your property and you are paying. Whenever I am having works done – assuming I am not living in the place at the time – I just go in at odd times, to let them know I am keeping an eye on things. If I find nobody there and that nothing has been done since my last visit, I call the main contractor to find out why – not in a nasty way, just in an enquiring way.

This strategy tells the builders that you are interested and concerned about the work, and are taking a close interest in it. You can also more easily correct small snags and mistakes along the way if you make frequent visits to the site. When you talk to the builders, ask them questions – don't ever be a know-all.

As a small woman, I often feel at a disadvantage when coping with 15-stone-plus builders. Here, it helps if occasionally I can take a big or tall man with me. Psychologically, builders as a race relate better to men than women and, if you are a lone woman supervising building works, it can often pay to have a large male friend to accompany you to the site on occasion. The more this man looks like a bouncer, the better.

A couple of cautionary tales

All this is absolutely true, but, beware! Hiring a project manager and paying his not inconsiderable bill does not always guarantee the success of the renovation, nor does it necessarily mean that the work will come in at or under budget. One young couple, Freddy and Rebecca, bought an unmodernized terrace house in north-west London. Because they knew that it would need to be completely gutted and rearranged, they decided to employ a project manager at £20 an hour. It was a complete, expensive, disaster. Freddy says:

> Because we both had full-time jobs and had never undertaken anything on this scale before, we thought that we would do the whole thing properly and have a project manager.
>
> The chap we engaged was recommended by a friend and he undertook to hire the builders and supervise every stage of the building process. I had already drawn up plans. We did not need planning permission, but did need to comply with building regulations as two supporting walls were going to be knocked down. We had to have RSJs in two rooms, but otherwise there was no structural work. In principle we didn't have to do anything. We were quoted a fixed price of £40,000, which was our total budget anyway for the job.

The project manager was supposed to give a weekly breakdown of costs, which Freddy and Rebecca paid in cash. Freddy said:

I was getting amounts like £10,000 out of the bank in cash and I'm sure the bank manager thought I was a drug dealer or something. In any case, major problems soon presented themselves. The building regs man came round and told us the lintel for the space between the two rooms was too small and did not fit in with current regulations. Our project manager had already bought the lintel without checking that it was the right size.

This meant that the floor had to be taken up and we had to cover these extra costs. Then we were told a trench had to be dug for a water pipe and this meant that the house was unsupported. We only became aware of it when we saw huge cracks in the downstairs bay window.

The project manager had ordered special radiators, then the radiator company went bust. We paid £3,500 for new floorboards that are not level. After they were sanded and varnished, water started to soak through.

Everything was going wrong and the job was going way over budget and over time. We could not live in the place while works were going on, but the worst thing was that I couldn't talk to the workmen because everything had to go through the project manager.

In the end, with the house still in chaos, Freddy and Rebecca sacked the project manager and Freddy supervised the work himself. 'I took three weeks off work to try and sort it all out and I must say the workmen were terrific. The brickies and the plumber became friends and the plumber felt so sorry for us he even did some work for nothing.'

Next time, says Freddy, he would take responsibility, and get more people to come round and estimate:

I would insist on a detailed written quote to make sure that costs didn't keep escalating.

We made the mistake of grabbing at the project manager because he was able to start work right away and we wanted to move in as soon as possible, especially as we were expecting our first baby, but now, looking back, I think that having a project manager takes away some of the satisfaction of a major renovation. When you do things yourself, it feels more yours.

When I went to see Freddy, he apologized for the lack of furniture: 'We can't afford any furniture at the moment and are making do with a few chairs. Our dining table is an old door supported on trestles.'

Next is another tale of woe concerning a project manager. Susan had three major jobs she wanted doing: building a two-bedroom cottage at the bottom of the garden (there was already a 40-foot disused warehouse there), extending a bedroom and addressing a severe dry rot problem that had appeared in the kitchen.

Because the house was Georgian, she took care to find a project manager who specialized in such properties. She found such a person through a friend, who would be responsible for the building regulations, architect and builder. He would also supervise all three projects.

Susan appointed him and let him get on with it. She says:

Each week I went to the site, handed over cheques and had a verbal update. At first, I thought I could not have anyone better looking after my interests – he was so reassuring – but, from this trusting and naïve position, horrendous problems occurred.

The project manager didn't believe in paperwork, so I have no paper trail. He failed to take out party wall awards on the grounds that this would delay things. When problems arose, he denied that he was the project manager and walked away from everything.

When I consulted my lawyers, it seemed that even invoices with the words 'project manager' on them are not enough to take legal action.

In Freddy and Rebecca's case, once the works were finished the couple were so traumatized they could not bear to live in the place, and sold it straight away. They said they hated the house – not because of the house itself, but because the major renovation had put them through more stress than they could comfortably handle.

How to avoid disaster

A good project manager is worth his or her weight in bricks and mortar, but a bad one is worse than useless. Complicated jobs do need project managing, but, before appointing anybody to do this vital job, make sure that they are what they say they are. As with builders, never grab the first person available.

Because project managing is not yet a 'real' profession, it attracts the charmers and the liars. This is not to defame the genuine people, but it is all too easy to impress people anxious to get on with the job. Before taking anybody on, ask to talk to their previous clients and see previous work. Also, insist that everything is put down on paper. As these last two cases show, it is sheer madness not to have everything written down and agreed to by both parties – in advance.

If you are the person paying, NEVER take your eye off the ball.

A surveyor

It is often said that it is essential to have an independent surveyor for major building projects, but this is no guarantee that things will run smoothly. Surveyors are expensive, but their one big advantage is that they must belong to a recognized professional association, so you have recourse to this if they do not do their job properly.

What they can do for you

You can appoint a surveyor in place of a project manager. The problem is that, like good builders, good surveyors are booked up for weeks, maybe months, ahead and the tendency always is to want the job done now. Although I said earlier that I believe full structural surveys are largely a waste of money, it is a completely different matter when the surveyor is actually going to work on your property.

Surveyors, on the whole, tend to be decent, professional, often slightly humorous people who are easy to get on with. Here is another piece of advice: if the specialist you are considering hiring does not resonate with you or your gut feeling is not positive, don't go with him or her. The relationship is likely to be long and difficult, so you should at least start off thinking along the same lines.

An interior designer

Some people imagine that it is unnecessary to retain a designer at an early stage, but I'm not so sure. The television image of interior designers is that they ponce around matching up this and that and acting in an outrageously camp fashion, but the good ones are in fact serious operators who can save you time, money and effort in the long run. Also, they are looking at homes day in, day out, so can often come up with ideas that would never have occurred to you.

My experiences

I have called in an interior designer for at least three renovations, long before building work has started, and it has always been worthwhile. My designer charges a day rate, as she does not do any of the actual work, but simply gives advice.

Architects will, of course, act as designers, but I'm thinking here of projects that do not need an architect. For instance, I once bought a maisonette in very bad condition. It did not need structural alteration, but was in such a mess that I did not know where to start or what to do. My designer friend advised me to paint all the walls white and carpet the entire place in beige before doing anything else. This, she said, would enable me to live in the house while I decided gradually what I wanted.

On another occasion, she gave me some quick, simple ideas on streamlining and colour coordinating the place so that, again, I could live with it before spending large sums of money that I might later regret.

In fact, in my own home I would always ask a designer to come and give me some quick, cheap tips for making the place habitable and aesthetically acceptable before ever embarking on major work. I would live for three years with an avocado bathroom before grabbing at a plumber just because he happened to be available.

The 'House Doctor' Ann Maurice is famous for giving people whose houses won't sell some low-cost ideas for tarting up and streamlining them. There are now companies that specialize in giving this kind of advice and very often they can earn their keep by giving you tips and hints on how to improve your home without spending a fortune.

Gavin's experience

Graphic designer Gavin Pretor-Pinney decided to employ an interior designer when he wanted to renovate his west London flat. Gavin had already lived in his flat for several years, so was not giving it a quick makeover having just moved in. He said:

> I had some idea of what I wanted, but did not know what would be possible or what it might end up looking like. I wanted to relocate the kitchen and bathroom and open up the kitchen into the living room, to provide entertaining space.
>
> The entire budget for this was £25,000, with the designer taking 12 per cent. For this, she drew up plans, found the builders and supervised the works. I knew that I would be no good at coordinating various tradespeople myself and I simply didn't have the contacts. Also, I knew it would stress me out too much.

For instance, says Gavin, you might know of one plumber, recommended by a friend, but if that plumber can't come, you probably can't find another, 'but my designer is using plumbers, electricians and so on all the time, so has a list of several.'

The other advantage of using an interior designer, says Gavin, is that they can see things you can't:

> When you are living in the place, you often can't get much perspective on how it could look. Yet it comes easily to professional designers to rethink spaces and know what can be done. My designer got in all the estimates and worked round my budget. She sourced the tiles I wanted and also advised on colour. For instance, I wanted white walls, but she felt that white would be too stark, so she mixed three-quarters white

with one-quarter cream to get a colour that looks white but is slightly softened down.

Five years after his renovation, Gavin is still delighted with the results:

> Designers know cheap ways round and they can often save you a lot of money. The other advantage is that you are shielded from the builder. Designers act as a buffer and I think this is a good idea, as builders tend to blind you with technical stuff you probably don't understand.
>
> After the work was finished I had the flat valued and it had definitely added much more value than the cost of the work. So it was money well spent.

Gavin believes that, when using a designer, it's essential to have a secret contingency fund: 'If the designer knows you've got the extra money, she will probably spend it, but, as things always, always go over budget, it's wise to have a 10–20 per cent contingency to pay for unseen extras.'

Some other benefits

Another plus point is that designers can help you avoid the 'developer' look, which is always such a turn-off. The expensive unsaleable house in my street that I mentioned in Chapter 1 had 'developer' written all over it. 'Developers,' said one local estate agent, 'cut corners all the time and always think they know everything.' Typical of the developer look are magnolia walls, endless seas of laminate flooring, kitchen islands (almost always a no-no in British houses), fake granite worktops, no storage and Venetian blinds. You almost never see any real style or luxury when a developer has been let loose on a property. Also, discerning buyers can always winkle out the developer look and will turn their noses up at it.

Whenever planning a significant alteration to a property – whether my own home or a buy-to-let property – I would always invite an interior designer in first, before starting work on it.

If a designer is not going to work on the project as such, but is there simply to offer advice, this means that they are not getting any kickbacks, nor do they feel any inclination to pull the wool over your eyes. I always reward my designer for her initial input by giving her the contract for curtains, blinds and any other soft furnishings when the building work has been completed.

There are now attempts to make the job of interior designer more professional. The British Interior Design Association has been created to promote high standards in a profession notorious for its laxity. Members of the BIDA must have a relevant degree or diploma, a minimum of six years' experience and a completed case history to present. They must also keep up to date with rules and regulations and take out professional indemnity insurance. Of course, membership of this organization does not necessarily guarantee chemistry between designer and client, but it is a start.

The British Interior Design Association can be contacted by phoning 020 7349 0800 or visiting its website at www.bida.org.

An electrician and plumber

What an electrician can do for you

Finding a good electrician is essential as we have so many electrical items in the home that we feel we cannot live without.

It is very important to call in a fully qualified electrician at an early stage as many old properties are full of dangerous outdated or DIY electrical systems, with circuits in danger of being overloaded and so on.

Surface trunking always looks horrible and is a sure sign that somebody, somewhere, has tried to save money on wiring. One of my properties has surface trunking and I hate it, but it was done many years ago and, now, to do away with these eyesores would mean stripping the walls back to plaster and rewiring the whole place. Even though it would look great, it would be too much work, expense, effort, dust and rubble for the result. In the meantime, too, the flat would be uninhabitable. So, I have decided to live with it. If you have a choice, though, make sure that wiring is embedded in the walls as surface trunking could well detract from the value of your property.

It is the job of a project manager to hire one or more electricians at an early stage and discuss with you where you want power points and sockets. However, many people simply don't know in advance exactly what they will need, where, so the best thing is to take advice from those who are dealing with wiring every day of the week. If you want an outside security light or, indeed, any outside lighting, discuss this at the same time as having any other wiring done.

Electricians will also let you know what kind of lighting you can and can't have. For instance, bathroom lighting has to be fully enclosed and is often of a low wattage, but there are various options, so ask. Similarly, many central light fittings do not give out much light and most lampshades only allow bulbs with a maximum wattage of 60, otherwise they burn out. Lighting is complicated, not always satisfactory and there are not always clever lighting solutions to everything. Personally, I like the option of having either an extremely bright light or a dim light, so I have dimmer switches wherever possible. Some types of light fittings are not suitable for dimmers, though, so it is not a universal solution.

The best idea is to tell your electrician what kind of lighting or what kind of light effects you are after and then he will tell you whether or not what you want is possible.

You can't have too many options for table lamps and floor lamps, to my mind, nor can you have too many power points. These should always be double ones and dotted around everywhere.

What a plumber can do for you

Fully qualified (CORGI-registered) plumbers are also essential if you are to have a fully functioning modern home. They, too, have to come in at an early stage. All good building firms should have lists of qualified electricians and plumbers whom they will usually subcontract. Again, this is something you must ask about before hiring a contractor. If you are expected to find your own electrician or plumber, do not use that firm.

There are two choices of boiler type for central heating systems: a standard one or a combi. The combi does not need a tank in the roof as it heats the water as required. Combi boilers are, to my mind, a significant advance on traditional boilers as they enable you to have hot water instantly, but are not heating water up when it is not needed. If you already have an ordinary boiler, it would be very expensive to replace it with a combi, but, if you are starting from scratch, I would always go for the combi.

Before any work starts, discuss with your builder whether or not it is possible to have another loo. In my view, you can't have too many and an extra loo in the cupboard under the stairs or an outside building will never be money ill spent. In some cases it will not be possible to have a standard loo, so you will have to have a Saniflo (macerator-type) one instead, which requires only a small-bore pipe. Macerator loos are useful as extras, but must never be the only loo in the property as this is not allowed by building regulations. Why? Because macerators work (if I can put it reasonably delicately) by grinding up the waste using electric pumps, so if there is a power cut, they won't work at all. Also, they are expensive to fit and *very* expensive to repair.

Some general advice

Whenever a good electrician or plumber enters your house, take his name and details at once, as I can guarantee you will always need him later. Never take on an electrician or plumber unless they are fully qualified, insured and members of their professional association. Otherwise, you may have no comeback.

Electrical and plumbing aspects of domestic renovation are very important in terms of safety, practicality and aesthetic considerations and you simply cannot afford to do these jobs on the cheap or by using unqualified operators.

A tiler

Tiling is a skilled job and definitely should not be done by amateurs. Never attempt tiling yourself unless you are a master tiler as it will look dreadful and detract from the final appearance of the job. Your builder should have tilers on call, but many builders include tiling among their skills.

Is it worth it?

Many people are horrified by the price of tiling, but it is labour-intensive – slow and laborious. Instead of skimping on tiling work, decide at the outset whether or not you really need it. It may not be necessary at all in a kitchen and how little can you get away with in a bathroom? This is a particularly important consideration when developing or buying to let as the price of tiling can add quite a large extra sum on to the job.

A useful piece of advice

When buying tiles, always buy quite a few more than you will need for the job. The reason for this is that even the plainest tiles may not be available several years later when you need some to replace ones that have fallen off or cracked. Even ordinary white tiles may be difficult to match up after a few years as the whites are not always the same.

A plasterer

Professional plasterers are fascinating to watch. They slosh buckets of plaster at a wall, smooth it over and, hey presto, within a very few days, the walls will be as smooth as satin. At least, they should be.

Plasterers are skilled craftsmen and in short supply, so they can name their price. Discuss with your builder what will need plastering and where you may be able to get away with plasterboard, which is much cheaper and easier to apply.

Plasterers, too, have to come in at the right stage of the work. They may well be subcontracted, so you need to know whether or not your specification includes the cost of plastering. Usually it will. Plastering will be needed wherever new walls or ceilings are being created.

A bricklayer

Bricklaying is a highly skilled job and good brickies are in very short supply. Whenever a new wall has to be built, make sure that your project manager, architect or designer can call on competent bricklayers at the right time to do the job. This is another aspect of renovation where you simply can't afford to compromise or go for cheap labour.

A carpenter or joiner

Most renovation jobs will involve some carpentry. Discuss with your builder who will be doing this and whether or not the quote includes painting and finishing and handles where required. Very often, prices are simply for the woodwork, not for painting or providing handles. It pays to check as, if you are having a bespoke wooden or MDF kitchen installed, for instance, you do not want to be left with unfinished units and cupboards simply because you did not realize that the quote excluded painting and decorating. It is usually the case that a decorator will be yet another tradesperson, as we shall see next.

A painter or decorator

A painter or decorator will come in last and pull the whole project together. Very often, a builder's quote will not include decorating and some do not get involved with this stage of the work at all.

Who will do the painting?

As said earlier, many builders do not quote for final painting and decorating and, while this makes the job seem cheaper initially, it leaves you having to find a decorator at the end of the job. If you go with a builder who does not quote for this work, make sure you have suitable people lined up, as to have this important work unfinished can cause much extra stress and worry.

Painting and decorating is a skilled job, if done properly, so it is important not to cut corners at this stage. Also, do make sure you have enough money in the budget for the painting work, as otherwise it will look forever unfinished.

Do I really need one?

As most renovators have run out of money by the time the painting stage is reached, the temptation is to do it yourself, on the grounds that 'anyone' can paint a wall. In fact, this is not strictly true. Amateurs rarely prepare surfaces properly and they often don't use the right kind of paint, either. Painting and decorating needs a lot of patience and, if you are not a patient, painstaking person, you may end up spoiling the final effect of all the hard work up to this point with an amateurish paint job. For instance, if walls have been newly plastered, they need to be sanded down and smoothed before painting and this is a time-consuming job. You also need to have a sander, but, if you don't have one, it may not be worth you buying it for one job.

In most cases, if you can't afford it now, it is worth waiting to have the job done professionally as it makes a dramatic difference. With painting and decorating, most of the cost is labour, which is why it is so tempting to do it yourself. The paint itself costs hardly anything in comparison.

Wallpapering also needs to be done by professionals, especially if you are using expensive wallpaper. Although wallpaper is much less popular than it used to be, it does have its place and, if walls are very uneven – as they may well be in an old property – lining or textured paper may be necessary.

Another argument against DIY is that, unless you do it regularly, you are unlikely to have the right equipment. So you have to go and buy brushes, rollers, dust sheets, ladders, papering tables, scissors, buckets and so on that you may use only once and where are you going to store it all when you've finished?

Other trades

You may also need to call on dry rot or damp specialists, flooring companies, roofers or glaziers. Sourcing all these people calls for research as anybody can set up in these trades without having any qualifications or, indeed, any expertise.

There is always the temptation to cut costs and let the builder lay the floor or put the glass in rather than hiring yet another specialist, but it may not be wise.

The golden rule is: make a careful note of all the various professionals who will be needed during the course of the work and make sure in advance that reputable people will be able to come on site when required.

Conclusion

When you take into account all the various professionals who are involved in the average renovation, you can see why it makes sense to do careful planning in advance. Most of the ancillary trades are paid a day rate, which, at the time of writing, is never less than £80 a day or £400 a week. Each.

This is why it is so important to be completely clear in your mind as to what the quote includes. People who are not used to renovation projects often assume that the quote includes everything, only to discover to their dismay that many essential elements are not included.

If, for instance, the quote does not actually specify painting and decorating, it's safe to assume that this is not included. My kitchen extension work did not include any decorating, but I persuaded a couple of the workmen to come in at weekends, for extra money, and paint the walls, ceiling and skirting boards. I'm glad I did as there was no way I could have done the work myself to a good standard.

Your relationship with the builders or professionals

This is a difficult one to get right. The standard course of such a relationship is that you start off friendly enough, then become extremely friendly and end up hating each other. To prevent this from happening, it is essential to establish boundaries from the start.

The best approach is to be businesslike and reasonably distant; polite, not too intimate or jokey. As you are spending huge sums of money and are likely to have your entire life disrupted for several months, it pays to remain cool and detached.

Lists and more lists

As work progresses, it is essential to make a daily list, then tick off jobs as they have been completed or as questions have been answered or problems solved. Also, write down anything that is bothering you and you need to check. Making daily lists like this keeps the whole thing on a professional footing and also lets the architect, project manager or site foreman know that you are keeping close tabs on everything.

These lists do not just have to contain 'snags' (things going wrong), but should also include everything you need to check and anything that is unclear to you.

What you should do and what they should do

Remember, all human beings thrive on praise, so praise any work you are genuinely pleased with. If you are not happy or are worried about any aspect, ask about it before blowing your top. There may be a simple answer as to why certain jobs don't appear to have been done or have been done in a particular way.

It is your job, as the client, to maintain a professional attitude. Do not get involved in making endless cups of tea and coffee for the builders, for instance. They should make their own plans for beverages.

The site should be left clean and tidy each night and disruption kept to a minimum. Make sure that they bring their own vacuum cleaner as they will ruin yours if they use it to clean up piles of dust and bits of brick.

Keeping things on an even keel

It is to be expected that strains in the relationship will develop as work progresses. Few people are prepared for just how much stress and trauma building work creates, whether this is in their own home or another property. So, before work starts, it is important to assess your own stress and temper levels – many renovation jobs are ruined by workers and clients losing their tempers with each other. It is so very common, especially as there is very often great stress from the builder's perspective as well.

Above all, keep lines of communication open. Builders themselves are not always very good communicators, but you as the client should certainly be. Ask about everything. Many clients don't ask essential questions because they don't want to seem ignorant, but there is nothing worse than pretending to know exactly what they are talking about when in fact, you know nothing.

The complaints procedure

Because all building work, even a seemingly straightforward job, requires a mass of complicated arrangements, things can and do go wrong. Property developer Ivan Twigden said, 'You never get everything right' and all builders – from international construction companies to a one-man band – would, if they were honest, agree.

So, what is the best approach to take when things go wrong? First of all, try communication and negotiation with your builder to see if matters can be put right amicably. Very often, getting satisfaction will be a simple matter of talking it through. If you are not happy with progress, ask your builder to explain why things are not further along. Then, if you are still not happy, you have a number of options:

▐ If your builder is proving incompetent, it may be best to cut your losses and sack him there and then.

▌ At this stage, many clients get on their high horse and instruct solicitors to sue the company. In most cases, this is an expensive hiding to nothing. There is little point in taking anybody to court unless you are pretty certain of winning. If your builder has no money anyway, it is a waste of time taking him to court. It is also highly likely that you will not have enough paperwork to satisfy lawyers or that there was not sufficient clarity in the original instructions to proceed satisfactorily down the legal route.

▌ Many building firms that proudly proclaim their membership of a professional association have merely paid an annual subscription fee. It is only worth embarking on legal action when the association concerned has a well set-up complaints procedure. If you are unhappy with a contractor who is a member of a recognized professional body, call this body and discuss your complaint. They may well be able to arbitrate.

▌ It is always acceptable practice to withhold the next tranche of money until the work has been completed as per the written agreement. A word of advice, though. If you are a lone woman tussling with a macho builder, try to have another man present with you. It's a sad fact that many builders talk to women in a way that they would not contemplate when dealing with a male client.

▌ Taking somebody to court is expensive, long-winded and may not lead to a satisfactory conclusion. In my experience, judges are peculiar creatures with all kinds of odd agendas going on inside their heads and you never know which way they may jump. Often, it seems to me, the person with the best or most persuasive team of lawyers is the one who comes out victorious, not necessarily the person who is right.

▌ Many how-to books on renovation advise going to the Citizen's Advice Bureau. In my experience, they do not have enough clout to achieve results as often as they would like.

So, if you're not satisfied, this is the procedure:

▌ Discuss the matter with your builder – it may be possible to sort it out amicably.

■ If he is a member of a recognized professional association, contact it and report the matter. If the association has a grievance procedure, it will set this in motion right away.

■ Do not pay any more money until the problem has been put right.

■ The fact is that most builders and contractors are not members of professional associations. If none of the above actions solve the problem, sack your contractor without further ado.

■ If you have a comprehensive paper trail – and only if – contact your lawyer to write a letter to your contractor asking for compensation or other satisfaction. Many builders are frightened of solicitors, while others are so used to solicitors' letters that they just ignore them.

■ Only ever consider taking somebody to court if all else has failed and the contractor is in a position to pay damages or compensation. Many work hand-to-mouth and so have no money – you can't get blood out of a stone.

■ Remember that legal procedures are all extremely stressful and only serve to increase your stress levels when they are at an all-time high anyway.

■ Make sure you know about the reputation of any building firms that you might employ in the future. Although there are always many things that can go wrong, a good builder will do his utmost to put them right, because not only does his reputation depend on customer satisfaction but also his self-esteem. Here is an example of a good builder. A few months after my conservatory extension had been completed, bad weather caused the wood to expand so that the doors were completely jammed. I called my builder, Anthony Green, and he was over the very next day to sort out the problem, which took several hours. Most reputable builders will do this as a matter of course. Another thing: never ever engage a contractor who only works from a mobile. You want to know that you can contact him if things go wrong when the job has been finished.

Part 2
Achieving successful transformations

4 Kitchens and bathrooms

Kitchens

In recent years, the kitchen has definitely become the heart of the home and, as with all hearts, it is difficult and expensive to operate on in terms of skills, equipment and appliances. Every kind of trade and skill is needed when constructing a kitchen – plumbers, electricians, carpenters, joiners, designers, plasterers, tilers, flooring fitters, bricklayers – and all have to come in at just the right time in the proceedings to create exactly the right result. Kitchens are just too complicated to do it yourself and, mostly, they need a specialist kitchen designer as well as the building trades mentioned above.

Because modern kitchens can easily cost up to £100,000 – indeed, the average price for a kitchen in the *25 Beautiful Kitchens* magazines is £57,000 all told – the whole thing has to be thought out very carefully before you start. Today's kitchens can be overly fussy and too designed and there is also a danger of incorporating too many gadgets and complicated appliances that, quite honestly, the average person will never use. As for 'adding value', there is not much point in installing a £50,000 kitchen to add £4,000 on to the value of your property. In fact, a £50,000 kitchen would rarely, if ever, put that much added value on to a property. The more expensive a kitchen is, the more likely it is to be very individual and therefore not appeal to all tastes. Also, like flash sports cars and yachts, flash kitchens date and depreciate extremely quickly.

Modern kitchens are high-cost fashion items, status symbols, which can either enhance or detract from the general appearance of your property. A 10-year-old kitchen, even a high-spec one, looks 10 years old and incorporates the tastes and ideas of a decade ago.

In 1988, I went to town and ordered an expensive, bespoke, hand-painted, rag-rolled kitchen with handmade tiles. It looked wonderful when newly finished, but I can't believe how old-fashioned it looks now. It's *so* eighties! In other words, if you want your kitchen to look high status, you have to keep changing it to keep up with the times – a very expensive and disruptive endeavour indeed.

In the United States, it's common for rich women to have brand new kitchens every few years, even when they have only made a cup of coffee in the old one. We haven't quite got to that point in the UK, but it's heading that way, so even high-quality kitchens are coming to be seen as throwaway or temporary items.

How long will a look last?

Professional interior designers say that any look, however cutting edge and trendy at first, is usually good for five years, after which it will start to look distinctly dated. Although there are looks that are more classic than others, even the blandest, most neutral type of interior can start to look old-fashioned eventually. Colours date, fabrics date, designs date and kitchens and bathrooms certainly date.

What happens is that an interior's look starts out being very upmarket but, before you know where you are, this look, or a version of it, has crept down the market so that eventually you are on a level with the cheapest and most readily available type of design. If you want proof of this, walk round Harrods, or another very upmarket retailer, and then take a trip to B&Q or Wickes – and you will see that many of the most upmarket ideas are already in these out-of-town outlets at bargain prices. Interior design nowadays follows much the same pattern as dress design, in that hot catwalk looks are in the downmarket shops in a matter of weeks.

Obviously a very expensive bespoke kitchen will never filter down to the mass market in its entirety, but elements of it will be incorporated into low-price equivalents.

For this reason, it is rarely these days (in my view) worth going for very, very expensive kitchens as you will simply not recoup the cost on resale. And after 10 years, it will look as old-fashioned as a cheap kitchen.

Planning to get the most from your new kitchen

Fashion item or not, bear the following points in mind when redesigning a kitchen, any kitchen, to ensure maximum appeal to homebuyers:

▌ **If the existing kitchen is very small, is there any way it could be made bigger?**
Could it be incorporated into the living area? Could it extend into the garden? Could any cupboards or walls be taken out to create extra space? The bigger your kitchen is, the better. Desirable modern kitchens have dining areas and entertaining space. The days when they were tucked away in servants' quarters are definitely over; now, they are meant to be on show. If you can't see a way of expanding your kitchen, it may well pay to have a specialist round to see how to maximize use of the available space. My own interior designer has often advised me on kitchens, long before I have contacted a kitchen firm.

A big kitchen is a greater selling point than an overtly designed kitchen. So, wherever possible, create a new kitchen that will provide a dining area and will not cut the cook off from guests. If there really is no way in which to enlarge the space, why not install a hatch? The kitchen hatch, popular in the 1970s, was an extremely useful idea – one that, to my mind, deserves to be brought back.

The most desirable kitchens of all are those that will seat 20 people for Christmas dinner, as well as a couple for an intimate evening – not easy to achieve, but what everybody would like in an ideal world.

▌ **If the existing kitchen is very dark, is there any way in which it could be made lighter?**
A kitchen with lots of natural light is a massive selling point. Could the window(s) be enlarged? Could a skylight be put in the roof? Could part of the kitchen have a glass roof? Whatever you can do to bring in more light to a dark kitchen will not only

add value, but also enhance your lifestyle in the meantime. If it is not possible to add natural light, find out about the best ways in which to improve the situation with artificial lighting. I would say that light and space are always essential.

I **Do you really need that island?**
If you are spending a lot of money creating more space, don't, whatever you do, lose it all by installing a massive kitchen island. If you look in kitchen magazines, you will see that almost all of the pictures show an island. This is a US idea that, in my view, rarely works in the UK as it cuts down entertaining and dining space. The exception to this is where a more modest island, or breakfast bar, creates a room divider and still leaves a large dining area. However, sitting up at a breakfast bar is vastly less comfortable and cosy than sitting round a dining table. If there is not room for both a massive dining table and an island, go for the big dining table every time – only consider an island where the kitchen is or will be absolutely vast.

I **Does your existing kitchen really need to be completely ripped out?**
Don't spend money unnecessarily. Dated kitchens can often be given a new lease of life by painting the existing units or by having new doors and handles put on to the existing carcases. Also, don't forget, what goes around, comes around. A once-dated 1970s kitchen can, 30 years later, look appealingly retro. Ditto a 1950s kitchen. You may only need to spruce it up and accessorize accordingly. There are now many kitchen door companies in existence, and you will see advertisements for them in the Sunday supplements and interiors magazines. These companies make the point that, by just fitting new doors, you can have what seems to be a brand-new kitchen at a fraction of the price of installing a completely new one. As all the carcases are the same, whether you buy cheap or expensive it can make sense just to fit new doors to update your kitchen. This means that the old kitchen will not have to be ripped out and remodelled at huge expense and disruption. But beware! These kitchen door companies, which are springing up all over the place and invite you to

send for a free glossy catalogue, are very pushy and hard-selling indeed. Within days of sending off for a catalogue, I was contacted by a salesperson wanting to fix up a time when a designer could come and visit. This was followed by at least 10 more calls from call centres, long after I had decided not to go for the doors but to have a complete new kitchen. My builder had advised that just having new doors wouldn't work, and he was right, as it turned out. Many of these kitchen door companies are a bit like timeshare in that they never leave you alone and they employ hard-selling techniques along the lines of double-glazing salespeople. If you are not certain of your ability to refuse one of these smooth-talking salespeople, leave them severely alone.

▌ **Do you need integrated appliances?**
These give a streamlined look as they are behind doors, but are they practical? They cost more than freestanding units and can be difficult to replace or repair. Certainly, when property developing or buying to let, make sure that the appliances are freestanding. Anyway, modern fridges and other appliances are often designer statements and look good so you should be able to see them. You may have less space in an integrated fridge, which is a drawback as the bigger the fridge, the more desirable it is. Wherever possible, do not situate fridges where you have to bend down to open them. Fridges should be at eye level, with the less often used freezer down below. Also, never place a washing machine where it will be difficult to extricate when repairing or replacing. I have viewed many new properties where the emphasis has been so much on design that you would have to dismantle the greater part of the kitchen to get at the back of the washing machine. I have also viewed many new build properties where you have to remove the kick board to pull out the washing machine. A kitchen needs to be practical as well as beautiful.

▌ **Is there anywhere for a utility or laundry room to go?**
Wherever possible, it is better to have washing machines and tumble-dryers in an area that is separate from the kitchen. In a

flat, this may not be feasible, but if there is a spare cupboard or
box room somewhere, investigate its laundry room possibilities before designing the new kitchen. If the kitchen is to
double up as a dining room, it is even more important to have
washing facilities elsewhere, if at all possible. Don't be
tempted to take away a downstairs cloakroom to do it, though.

▌ **Think hard about storage**
This is especially important for such items as the ironing
board, a stepladder, vacuum cleaner, cleaning products, dirty
laundry and rubbish. In some overly designed kitchens these
practicalities have clearly not been thought about. A good-
looking kitchen is one thing, but it needs to be a practical
working space first.

▌ **What price level of kitchen are you considering?**
Do not ever install a kitchen to a higher or lower specification
than the general value of the property. A high-value property
should have a high-value kitchen and vice versa.

▌ **What about colour?**
Neutrals work best, every time. Kitchens shown on television
programmes are often very colourful, indulging the whim of
the owner for shocking pink, midnight blue or whatever. They
look dramatic, but, in my view, colourful kitchens are not a
good idea as you spend so much time in them that you soon
tire of the colour. Also walk away from pink fridges, dark-red
Agas and so on, however tempting they look – particularly an
Aga as that really is a permanent item. Although they look
exciting at first, colourful units and appliances eventually pall
and the colours date. Drama and interest can be added with
tablecloths, crockery, pictures and curtains instead. I once
inherited a scarlet kitchen and the first thing I did was to paint
all the red units a very pale blue. Instantly, the kitchen looked
twice the size and much more modern. Gimmicky colours and
designs are to be avoided; restrain yourself.

▌ **Does the kitchen actually need tiling?**
This is always expensive and, surprisingly quickly, the grout
becomes dirty and dingy. Also, you will most probably not be

able to replace the tiles later if they break or become loose. In general, tile patterns and designs only stay on the market for two years before being discontinued. Splashbacks are essential, but these days can be made of glass, stainless steel or acrylic – they do not have to be tiled.

▌ **Is there space for a cooker hood and ducting?**
Although not essential, ducting an extractor through an outside wall adds value and makes the kitchen a more pleasant place to work in.

Money matters

When pricing a kitchen, add up *all* the figures before you begin – including the kitchen designer, painter and decorator and new crockery, cutlery and so on. The price of the units is only the start. You also need to know how much it will cost to demolish the existing kitchen, what electrical, plumbing, plastering and other initial work is needed, how much any alterations will cost and how much it will cost to install the new kitchen. Make sure that you work all these figures out very carefully *before* you start. It sounds obvious, but most people don't as they are eternally optimistic (and unrealistic) about the true cost of home renovation.

Complying with rules and regulations

You need to know well beforehand whether or not any projected works require planning permission or building regulations approval. For instance, if you are developing an apartment in a block, you may need to have fire and smoke alarms, double-glazing and sound insulation. If you are dividing a house into flats, these works are essential. Also, before starting work in an apartment, check that everything you are considering is allowed in the lease. If the building is listed or in a conservation area, there may well be tight restrictions on windows, ducts, flooring and ceilings. Also, in listed buildings, inside alterations need planning permission just as much as outside work.

One friend bought two studios in a listed London block, then proceeded to knock them into one, larger flat. It never occurred to her to seek permission for these alterations, but she was taken to court by the landlord and ordered to reconvert them back into studios, at huge expense to herself.

Never ignore rules and regulations. Building restrictions are getting tighter all the time, so you may have to observe energy-saving rules, soundproofing rules and safety rules. As well as being the most expensive, kitchens are also potentially the most dangerous rooms in a property. Most house fires start in kitchens. Every safety feature you are required by law to incorporate will cost yet more money.

Everything and the kitchen sink

Then, there will be the cost of the new sink, appliances, flooring, tiling (though, see above) and redecoration. Also, take into account how much the labour will cost, not just the prices of the items themselves. If developing for profit, you also need to know how long it will all take, as time is money. For instance, do the taps you particularly want have to be specially ordered from Italy or are they in stock at the warehouse? Try to arrive at a total price for the finished kitchen, including any lighting, gadgets and furniture, before starting, then double it. Then allow a reasonable amount of time for the works to be carried out.

On television, it is all a rush against time. It is common for presenters to say, 'Mr and Mrs X have given themselves a budget of £200 and a timescale of four weeks to renovate this kitchen', but, in real life, you have to assume that the work is going to cost twice as much and take twice as long as you were led to believe.

There's no such thing as a free lunch

The kitchen industry is extremely competitive and there are some very high-pressure sales techniques around. Most kitchen sales-people are on commission, so be aware of this when looking round. Do not ever be seduced by cold callers saying that they are 'in your area' or leaflets pushed through the door offering a kitchen at a fraction of the true cost if it can be used as a show kitchen for future customers. Do your own research, your own planning.

Even the cheapest kitchen works out expensive by the time you have finished, but there is no doubt that a really lovely, well-designed kitchen is a greater selling point than any other aspect of a modern property.

Overcoming kitchen challenges

The biggest challenge with a kitchen is to make it up to date, state of the art, cutting edge and so on, yet remain in keeping with the property itself. For instance, Victorian and Georgian houses generally need traditional-looking kitchens that nevertheless operate as modern kitchens. A 1930s home usually looks best with an art deco kitchen and a new build property with a very contemporary kitchen. The possibilities are endless, but putting in the wrong style of kitchen for your home is a very expensive mistake and not easy to rectify.

If the kitchen is going to be part of the dining or living room, you don't want it looking too kitcheny. Wooden or hand-painted kitchens with wooden worktops look best where they are going to be permanently on show and have to blend in with other furniture.

Granite and marble worktops give a luxury finish, but can look cold and forbidding in the wrong setting. Make sure that the worktop you choose is easy to keep clean and not difficult to maintain.

Handles can date very quickly, but they are easily replaceable, unlike worktops.

Kitchens for developing and buy-to-let properties

Here, you are looking for the cheapest and quickest solutions without wanting to look like a cheapskate.

When renovating for profit, the kitchen has to appeal to the widest possible tastes, but this should always include space for eating, if possible, a dishwasher (you can get small dishwashers if necessary), a washing machine, cooker, fridge-freezer, base and wall units. Washing machines and dishwashers should not be trapped inside units, but must be able to be pulled out easily for repair and replacement. Never put integrated appliances in a buy-to-let property, even a very upmarket one.

Buy-to-let properties will need the kitchens replacing every few years as they generally suffer a great deal of wear and tear. It is unlikely that a kitchen in a rented property will last more than 10 years. There is also not a lot of point in buying expensive appliances, as these will most probably be misused as well.

Flooring in a buy-to-let property has to be appropriate to the target market. Generally speaking, you can't beat vinyl, which is hardwearing, soft underfoot, reasonably cheap and easy to replace. Laminate kitchen floors can look extremely scruffy after a very short time and are now a bit cliché. In flats, laminate and wooden floors may not be allowed in the lease.

I would advise not to indulge your personal taste when renovating for profit. Instead, research your target market and aim hard at that, without deflecting from your purpose. Bear in mind that cheap units work just as well as expensive units as the carcases are very similar – it is the doors and finish that make the difference.

Worktops are a contentious area. For buy-to-let properties, unless they are extremely high spec, I would not go for granite, marble, wood or other expensive material. Worktops are expensive and can be difficult to replace, yet may need to be replaced in a rented property. Sinks should be stainless steel, as these are relatively easy to keep clean and replace. Expensive sinks are a waste of money.

Whatever the price or budget, I would always have the kitchen designed by an expert. Most kitchen companies now have designers and, if you go into the showroom with the measurements, they will design a kitchen to fit your space. They often come up with good ideas that have not occurred to you (see Figure 4.1 for examples of good kitchen layouts). Many mass-produced kitchens are very good looking and perfectly adequate for rental properties.

When kitting out such a property, you need a kitchen where everything is easily replaceable. So, do not be tempted to buy an end-of-line kitchen in a sale.

When renovating for profit, the secret is to be aware of your target market all the time. Professional property developers design kitchens to meet the requirements of an exact market and you have to do the same. To get the idea, visit some brand new developments, look carefully at the show home and note the

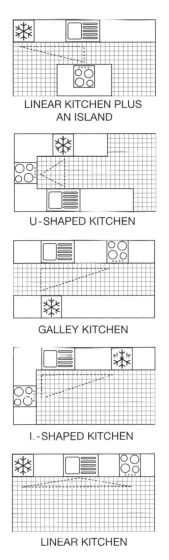

LINEAR KITCHEN PLUS
AN ISLAND

U-SHAPED KITCHEN

GALLEY KITCHEN

L-SHAPED KITCHEN

LINEAR KITCHEN

Figure 4.1   Examples of good kitchen layouts

quality and style of the appliances and finish in the kitchen. You
will see that the kitchen, above all, is designed to appeal to the
main potential market, whether that is the over-55s, young
families, young single professionals, second-homers or high-
earning couples.

The very small kitchen

Where space is at an absolute premium, you may like to consider a mini-kitchen, which is, typically, a complete unit with sink, work surfaces, a couple of wall units, a cooker, hob and small fridge. These fit into surprisingly small spaces – even a cupboard or former pantry. They are a very good idea when planning studio flats or turning an attic into a self-contained unit, for instance. If your property is big enough for a guest suite or annexe, it is worth considering installing a mini-kitchen as this enables guests to be self-contained, make themselves breakfast, a cup of tea and so on without bothering you.

Many companies now produce mini-kitchens. Ikea has lots of ideas for multifunctional rooms and its showrooms have imaginative room sets that can show you how to make the best use of a small space. Don't forget that, in the UK, the housing market is particularly short of affordable, self-contained single units. This is despite the fact that most people, apart from students, prefer to have a self-contained space to call their own. So, when developing, bear in mind that two studio flats are likely to be more popular and lucrative than a large, two-bedroom one aimed at young professionals sharing.

In the novels of Barbara Pym, set in the 1950s, genteel single ladies of a certain age were always having to share bathrooms and sometimes kitchens in their bedsits. Those days are over. The era of the single, self-contained unit has arrived, and mini-kitchens make the whole thing feasible.

Where there is no room for a dining table, a trolley on wheels is a good idea in a small kitchen, as it can act as extra storage and also a table to sit at with a cup of coffee and the newspaper.

Made-to-measure and bespoke kitchens

Companies such as Smallbone, Mark Wilkinson, John Lewis of Hungerford and a host of others will design and hand-build a kitchen just for you. They offer a much more personal and individual service than just a computerized design at a desk in one of the edge-of-town superstores.

Designers from bespoke kitchen companies try to accommodate your every whim and so will come round to measure up, find out exactly what you are after and offer advice. Of course, this kind of service comes at a (very high) price and is only worth it when the value of the property is high and where a truly lovely kitchen will add a large amount to the selling price.

The magazine *25 Beautiful Kitchens* advises customers never to commission a kitchen company to design your dream kitchen over the phone or via the internet. They say, 'It is essential to meet the designer face to face to see if you click.' Before you meet the designer, draw up a wish list for your kitchen and then see what is possible and practicable. All reputable kitchen designers should be members of the Kitchen and Bathroom Specialists Association (KBSA – which can be contacted on 01905 726066).

With bespoke kitchens, several home visits may be necessary and, as with other work, you will need to ask what is included in the price. Is labour included? Do they supply the team? Do they come and dismantle your old kitchen? Do they undertake decorating? Are appliances included in the price? Some kitchen companies exclude certain essential elements, such as plumbing – probably for fear that customers would keel over with shock if they were to give a final total price for the finished job, including light fittings, flooring, blinds or curtains, dining table, chairs and so on.

When renovating for your own purposes, you can go to town as much as you like, but even then it is important not to go over the top and install a kitchen that looks far too important and grand for the property itself. Avoid the baronial look, for instance, except in baronial properties.

The bespoke kitchen business can be risky and many firms go out of business. For this reason, stick with a tried and trusted kitchen retailer that has been in business for many years. The expert advice is to never give an advance deposit to a company that does not belong to the KBSA, as you may have no comeback if the firm goes out of business before work starts. This scenario is by no means unknown.

Some years ago, a few kitchen companies gave customers a guarantee that, after 10 years, their old kitchen would be replaced with a new one, free of charge, so long as all original receipts were kept. However, when the 10 years were up, none of those kitchen companies could be found. Don't make your decision based on any such schemes.

Off-the-peg kitchens

There is nothing wrong with these, but you do have to do more work yourself, such as assembling the team of workers to fit your kitchen.

Although most retailers selling mass-produced kitchens do offer a fitting service, there is often an 8- to 10-week wait and the fitting service is just what it says – a fitting service. It does not include plumbing or electrical work, redecoration or flooring.

Mass-produced kitchens may not quite fit, in the same way that mass-produced clothing may not fit you quite as well as an individually tailored suit. However, the mass-produced versions are usually near enough and computerized designs are extremely cleverly done to allow for this. Also, if you have a good team of builders on board, they can make clever use of odd little spaces here and there.

Some companies producing budget kitchens give you a square of graph paper and ask you to fill in your own measurements. There is much margin for error here and, as even a cheap kitchen works out expensive in the end, it is best left to the experts. If you take the floor measurements of your room, as accurately as possible, indicating where the windows and doors are, the computer will do the rest.

I have had several kitchens designed by computer in the showroom and they have worked out extremely well. They cost about an eighth of the price of a bespoke kitchen and, if you choose the design carefully, look nearly as good.

Some final tips

Whatever type of kitchen you go for, make sure that you get guarantees for all the appliances. This is particularly important when property developing. Do not fall for 'extended warranties' – in my view, they are a total waste of money.

In kitchens, more than any other room, the finish is all important as even the most expensive kitchens become scruffy in time. Make sure yours doesn't start off scruffy. Insist on a quality finish with your builders and, as with other building works, make a daily list of questions you need to ask, jobs that need doing and work that remains undone or unfinished. You can never abdicate responsibility with kitchens and your input is at least as important as that of those assembling your kitchen.

Finally, how long should kitchens last? Manufacturers say 10 years, but I have known kitchens last 30, 40 years or more. Appliances may need to be replaced, but there is no real reason for a good, well-fitted kitchen not to last forever – that is, except in a rental property, where it becomes dilapidated very quickly as a result of the high turnover of occupants. Also, the plainer the kitchen is to start with, the longer you (and subsequent occupants) will be able to live with it.

Bathrooms

Next to the kitchen, the bathroom is the most problematic part of a home to renovate, with many decisions to make that cannot be easily reversed or altered later. Although bathrooms are not *quite* as important as kitchens, they can be just as difficult to design and fit. As with kitchens, the bill for a new bathroom can be extremely high.

Modern bathrooms can be built into rooms, as in hotels, rather than be separate rooms and even quite small spaces can be turned into en suites, so long as the structure of the building enables pipework to deal with hot and cold water and waste. If you are property developing, don't forget that a macerator-type loo cannot be the only toilet available.

How many bathrooms do you need?

In general, the more bathrooms and shower rooms the better, so long as you do not take away a bedroom to put one in. (This rule may not apply in an eight-bedroom mansion, but it would not be sensible to take a bedroom away in a three-bedroom house.)

The Secret to The Perfect Wet Room Lies Behind The Tiles

Probably the simplest and most effective way to create a perfect, trouble free, designer wet room is to use the Kaskade shower tray in conjunction with No More Ply tile backer boards.

The Kaskade shower tray is a unique tray that can be used with confidence in a timber or concrete floor to form the wet room without a step that you've always wanted.

No More Ply is the ultimate tile backer board available from tile shops nationwide. Moisture proof, easy to handle, easy to cut, easy to lay on floors, easy to fix on walls. Very cost effective.

For more details phone **0800 0015 092**

There is much emphasis on having an en suite bathroom, but in a small house or flat with few occupants, an en suite is only recommended if it does not take away valuable space for storage, double beds and general living.

Bath or shower?

In properties aimed at families, a bath is essential, as small children cannot cope with a shower. In bachelor pads, showers alone are fine as very few men ever use a bath, even when there is one. Similarly, in properties designed for older people, you may be able to get away without having a bath as the over-55s increasingly prefer showers or wet rooms to baths. This may be because, as people get older, they may not be able to physically get into, let alone out of, a bath. For the older market, it is definitely worth considering putting in a wet room.

Where there is room, having a bath and separate walk-in shower is a good idea. Otherwise, make sure that if you put in a shower unit over a bath, it is the most powerful you can get. How powerful it is, though, will depend to some extent on the general plumbing arrangements, so check with your plumber as to what can be done.

What type of shower?

Essentially, there are two types of shower available: those that work independently and those that draw water off the main heating system. In my view, there is a lot to be said for the independently operating electric shower type as this means that you have instant hot water whenever required, rather than having to wait for water to be heated up by the boiler. Interior designers tend to turn their noses up at electric showers, believing them to be a design anachronism. Check out what the water pressure is and discuss the pros and cons of the different options with your plumber – you might be able to have the sleek designer look you're after or, if you don't have a high pressure system and a modern boiler, it might just drive you mad.

Your plumber also needs to inspect all the existing plumbing arrangements carefully in order to advise you what can and can't be done with bathrooms and showers and give you an idea of how much it is likely to cost. Adding more bathrooms and showers could mean that you need a completely new heating system and this could cost up to £8,000 before you start.

At this point, let me share a personal story. I originally wanted a shower unit when converting an outbuilding into a guest suite. I could have had a macerator-type loo, hot water and washbasin for under £1,000, but to provide enough power for a shower unit I would have had to upgrade the entire heating system, at a cost of £8,000, minimum. I decided that, on balance, it was not worth it.

There is a vast range of showers available and most of them work perfectly well for many years. Many of them are very complicated, multifunctional affairs, but only fit these in properties aimed at rich young professionals who enjoy twiddling lots of knobs. Cheap showers are perfectly adequate in cheap properties. If you are aiming the renovation at older people, keep it simple as, generally, they do not like having to cope with complicated technology that was not around in their young day.

Glass door or shower curtain?

The decision as to whether to fit a glass shower panel or a curtain on a rail is one of personal preference and there are pros and cons to each. Glass panels need to be cleaned all the time, especially in hard water areas, and they can bang against the basin in small bathrooms. Shower curtains come in a huge range of styles and prices and are easy to replace. Some people think shower curtains look pretty; others that they look messy. Whatever your view, just make sure the shower rail is strong and securely fitted. Get this fitted by an expert – unless you're handy, it's not suitable as a DIY project. This is particularly important in a buy-to-let property as a flimsy shower rail can easily be pulled down by tenants.

Is the bathroom warm enough?

In my view, the main problem with private bathrooms in the UK (as opposed to those in hotels) is that they are far too cold. Heated towel rails and bathroom radiators may belt out heat and, yet, in winter, the bathroom can still feel cold. People often forget, when designing bathrooms for eye appeal, that every single day users will be stepping out of the bath or shower dripping wet and naked.

How to address the heat issue? If your bathroom is cold even with a radiator and/or heated towel rail, the only way is to have a wall heater, which provides instant heat and operates separately from the main heating system on a pull switch. I have installed wall heaters in three bathrooms now and the bliss of having the bathroom warm enough more than makes up for their looking slightly naff. Don't assume that radiators and towel heaters will necessarily provide enough heat, especially as they are usually connected up to the general heating system. You want the bathroom to have the ability to be stifling and wall heaters may be the only way to achieve this.

Whenever you are having a bathroom renovated, ask about dry underfloor heating. These systems are now being extensively advertised as being space-saving, easy to install and cheap to run. All you need, so the advertising spiel goes, is one box! In particular, underfloor heating systems are being targeted at bathrooms – 'heat up your bathroom floor' – and many are aimed at small rooms or specific areas such as bathrooms, kitchens and conservatories.

They are, so the manufacturers promise, invisible and maintenance-free and they avoid the need for space-consuming radiators. They are electric, work by radiant heat and, at the time of writing, the systems cost from £300.

If interested in this form of heating, ask your contractor before having the bathroom installed as it may not be possible afterwards. Not all floors are suitable for underfloor heating, but it is a modern solution highly recommended for rooms where you may not want the entire central heating system on. Although they are advertised as being easy to install, this must be carried out by a qualified electrician, and be part of a general renovation project. In other words, the installer would have to liaise with your plumber so as to make sure it is installed at exactly the right stage in the proceedings.

Lighting

Lighting can be difficult in bathrooms, as units have to be enclosed, meaning that 60 watts is usually the maximum wattage allowed. Where possible, recessed lighting is the best answer in a bathroom. If the ceiling is extremely high, you may have to go for a fluorescent fitting, just to get enough light. To avoid this, perhaps the ceiling could be lowered to provide space for recessed lighting. Lower ceilings look cosy in bathrooms – high ceilings are almost always a mistake as they make the room seem out of proportion.

A light over the basin is a must for putting on make-up or shaving. Think, too, about whether or not you want a shaver unit or an electric toothbrush point. If so, these decisions have to be made and acted on at an early stage. Also, before deciding on a design, get an electrician to tell you what is and is not possible with lighting and heating arrangements.

Storage

Ideally, bathrooms should have enough space to be able to accommodate the laundry basket and storage of towels. If there is room for a cupboard in the bathroom, go for it. Also, think about storage for cleaning materials, toiletries and medicines. You can get lockable bathroom cabinets and these are often advised, but what if you lose the key? Again, keep it simple. Bathroom cabinets come in a vast range of sizes and prices and can add a lot to the total price. The large DIY stores have a good range and Ikea stock self-assembly cabinets that are cheap to buy, but do the job very well.

If there is room for an easy chair in a bathroom, this can add style and comfort. However, do not take up space in a bathroom that is better employed elsewhere.

How many bathrooms?

It is generally assumed that the more bathrooms, the better – especially when it comes to selling. I have viewed many apartments in the United States advertised as 'one bed, one and a half bathrooms'. This usually means that there is a cloakroom containing a loo and basin as well as the main bathroom and, although at first I thought it was over the top, I can now see the sense of it.

When marketing to families, it is a good idea to have an en suite bathroom for Mum and Dad and a family or guest bathroom that is not en suite. However, in a five-bedroom home, I would not reduce the number of bedrooms to four just to have an en suite. You may not be allowed by the planning department to site a bathroom at the front of the house, especially if this means soil pipes being visible from the front.

Loft conversions will always need an en suite shower room plus loo. If there is no possibility of having an extra bathroom in the loft, don't do the conversion in the first place. It's a waste of money.

In houses, a downstairs loo is an excellent idea. If you have an outbuilding or summerhouse, see if you could add a loo there as well. It is a magnificent selling point and will improve your quality of life. Outside and downstairs loos must also have hand basins. These can be very small indeed, but must be there. If there is not room for even a tiny hand basin, don't go to the expense of the loo. Macerator (Saniflo) loos are very expensive, both to install and repair, but can be a godsend.

Practical considerations

When renovating or redesigning, always make sure that there is enough room for a man six feet tall or more to stand up when using the loo. Some developers forget this, and situate en suite loos under sloping roofs – especially in loft conversions – with the result that only a male child will be able to use it in the customary manner. One very expensively renovated house I viewed did not sell because there was no way an adult man could use the loo in the loft conversion standing up. The developers in this instance were all men, so how they could have made this mistake is beyond me.

Any bathroom or cloakroom without a window will need ventilation. Make sure that a ventilation duct can be routed to an outside wall. Building regulations insist that even new bathrooms with windows should have a fan and I think this is a good idea.

Bathrooms can easily be spoilt by condensation. This problem can be avoided by fitting ventilators, which are reasonably cheap and obtainable from most ordinary electrical shops. However, they do need to be fitted by a qualified electrician.

Walk-in baths and baths specially designed for the disabled do limit your market if you are renovating for profit. Seeing all kinds of grab handles and so on will put non-disabled buyers off. Of course, if you are developing a property specifically for the retired market, this is a different matter, but, otherwise, go for a standard bath and fittings.

Bidet?

No. Even the French are abandoning bidets and you rarely see them in new developments. They are a waste of time, money and space.

Bathroom design

As with kitchens, the bathroom sector of the market is very competitive and a new bathroom suite can cost anything from £200 to six figures. The secret is to make sure that the quality of the bathroom reflects the general value of the property (see Figure 4.2 for some ideas on how to use space effectively). In cheap properties, acrylic baths from the big DIY stores are perfectly adequate. With expensive bathroom suites, you are paying for the look and the finish. The innards of a budget loo are very similar to the innards of an expensive designer version.

Plumbing arrangements have to meet British standards and, more than any other room, the bathroom needs to be installed by a totally competent plumber. It is worth spending time finding one who is CORGI-registered. It is a false economy to stint on the plumber as bathrooms must work, not leak.

When developing or renovating a buy-to-let property, the bathroom suite should always be white and of the simplest design you can find. The watchwords are sleek, smart, easy to operate, efficient and warm.

If the new bathroom is for your own home, then you can go to town, but I would never have a really big bathroom. They can be

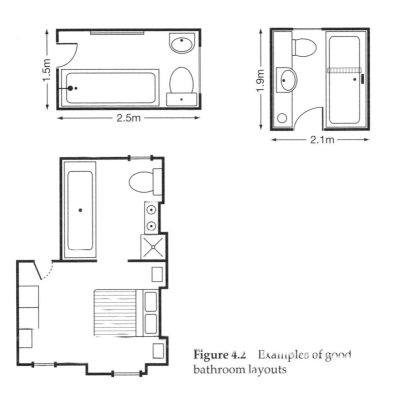

Figure 4.2   Examples of good bathroom layouts

difficult to heat sufficiently and waste a huge amount of space. If the room to be used as a bathroom is huge, why not consider hiving off some of it for a walk-in wardrobe, as they have in the United States?

Cast iron or acrylic?

More and more manufacturers are making acrylic baths and abandoning steel and cast iron. Cast iron baths are extremely heavy and, in an apartment block, the floor may not be strong enough to cope. Acrylic baths used to be definitely second best, but the designs and stability have improved greatly in recent years. In fact, many reputable bath manufacturers are no longer producing metal baths at all. Acrylic baths can scratch and, if you go for acrylic, make sure that the bath is strong enough to cope with a 16-stone user, plus the weight of the water.

If your property has an old cast-iron bath, it may not need to be replaced, but can be re-enamelled instead so that it looks brand new. This process is expensive and puts the bath out of use for a week, but is still cheaper and easier than taking it out, for which you will require four strong men.

Money no object

Very high-spec bathroom options include baths, basins and shower trays made from teak, transparent baths and glass basins, shower curtains that come down at the touch of a button and all kinds of gimmicks. When designing a high-spec, 'wow factor' bathroom, ask yourself whether or not you will tire of the gimmicks in a few years' time and if all the electronic controls will continue to work well as time goes on. Also, check which items are replaceable. Whirlpool baths and other complicated arrangements, for example, may just mean that there is more to go wrong, more to fiddle with.

Some simple rules of thumb

As with kitchens, do not order bathrooms over the phone or via the internet. Do not let yourself be seduced by cold callers either. In general, bathrooms do not need as much design input as kitchens – there are fewer items to incorporate and, usually, not much choice as to where each can go. Whereas kitchen designers are a necessity, most ordinary builders can design perfectly good bathrooms.

Whatever your needs and budget are, you can't go wrong if you keep it plain and keep it simple. If you want to add drama and impact, you can do this with shower curtains, pictures, wonderful toiletries, lovely towels and soaps.

Tiling

All bathrooms need some areas to be tiled, but keep this to a minimum and, again, keep it simple. Complicated, handmade tiles can be very tempting, but they soon date and may be unobtainable in a few years. Tile patterns have a very short shelflife indeed so, in any case, always buy more tiles than you need so that you have some ready as and when you need to replace them.

Tiling should never be amateurishly done as good tiling makes even cheap, simple bathrooms look smart and inviting.

Flooring

As with kitchens, a huge variety of bathroom flooring is available, from limestone to quarry tiles, ceramic tiles, vinyl, wood, lino, carpet. I would avoid both wood (or laminate) and carpet in bathrooms and only go for ceramic tiles if the floor will never need to be taken up to adjust pipework and so on. Indeed, never bury pipework that may need to be reached at some point.

There are some lovely vinyl floorings available, particularly the expensive Amtico ranges (and similar) and, in my view, you can't beat it. Old-fashioned lino is also a possibility, although this is not as malleable as vinyl and can be expensive.

Whatever you go for, choose a colour and design of flooring that is waterproof, easy to clean and hardwearing.

Selling on

If you are renovating to sell on or property developing, do not make the mistake of over-egging the pudding regarding kitchens and bathrooms. Estate agents are always nervous about telling people to improve their properties for selling purposes, but there is little doubt that a smart, clean, new kitchen and bathroom will help to sell a property.

The only problem is, will the new rooms add more value than it cost you to put in the kitchen and bathroom? Nobody can say for sure, but the expert advice is to make the kitchen and bathroom appeal to the widest possible taste. In fact, you can hardly be *too* simple when renovating for selling purposes. The simpler, the better as the designer kitchens featured in magazines do not suit everybody. You can't go wrong with a plain white kitchen (no island unit!) and plain white bathroom suite with plain white tiles and a white or pale floor.

When decorating for selling purposes, keep all the colours neutral and resist any temptation to put in strong colours, even if the whole thing looks completely bland to you. When I bought a rental flat, the newly installed (not by me) kitchen was all white. The tiles, floor, sink, units – even the white goods – were white and it looked just too bland, so I painted the walls and ceiling in a warm, saffron colour.

Your buyers can do the same. The important point is that it's easy to change the colour of the walls, if they like, but it's not so easy to change kitchen units or a bathroom suite and most buyers will not be prepared to do so. Keep it simple and unpretentious and you'll have a queue of potential buyers.

Louisa Fletcher, who founded the Property Price Advice website, disagrees with the prevailing wisdom that an uncluttered, clean and tidy property inevitably fetches a higher price than one that is badly presented. Her view, backed up by meticulous financial research, is that a dingy, cluttered property will inevitably take longer to sell than a smartly presented place, but that painting and decorating and adding new kitchens and bathrooms may not greatly increase the value.

In any case, you want to make sure you do not spend more on the renovation than is realized in extra value. The studio flat that I renovated at a cost of £11,000 added – at best – £15,000 to the asking price. So I had to ask myself: is it worth spending £11,000 to add at most an extra £4,000 on to the value? The answer has to be no – not really.

Most experts agree that a property in pristine condition will sell more quickly, but it may not sell for appreciably more, which in a sense gives the lie to all those property renovation programmes on television. If you look closely, you will see that the increased value often depends on a rising market.

But over and above this, there is the self-esteem factor. Although I might have only added £4,000, at best, to the value of my flat, I had made it into something I was proud of, rather than ashamed of. There are many wild cards in property renovation and the trick always is not to spend more than you can afford, or an amount that will cause you sleepless nights. Sometimes it is better to take a lower price for the sake of getting rid of a property. Not all properties may be good buys and it is silly to throw good money after bad.

5 Adding on – conversions, conservatories and extensions

Dr Madsen Pirie, of the Adam Smith Institute, believes that people should be encouraged to increase the living space of their existing homes with attic or basement conversions or conservatories and kitchen extensions rather than spending huge sums of money on moving. He is of the opinion that governments should facilitate this by zero-rating VAT on such improvements, as this would not only reduce pressure on land for new building but also generate huge numbers of jobs in the building industry. All this prompted some wisecracker to wonder if he should found the 'Conservatory Party'.

Some food for thought

A few years ago, most people would have moved house if they'd wanted to have more space, but now adding on, up or down is becoming a viable, and often cheaper, alternative to moving. A sign of this change in attitude struck me as I was sitting in a coffee bar attached to the offices of a branch of Abbey. All around the walls were posters inviting customers to borrow money for loft conversions, extensions and other home improvements.

Move or improve?

What are the considerations to bear in mind when wondering whether to move or improve?

If you have a family, a major factor is the garden, or lack thereof. Although you can go up, down and sideways, it is very rarely possible to increase the size of the garden, and families need gardens. If you only have a tiny garden, patio or balcony, it would certainly be better to move than to spend money on add-ons. In my view, a large garden is an absolute essential for families, as otherwise everybody goes stir-crazy. When the children grow up and move away, the garden may become a burden – and then perhaps it is time to downsize.

You also have to think about whether your projected add-on, such as a loft extension, would make the house darker and more cramped as regards landings and stairs, bearing in mind that light, light and more light is what people want these days.

A third factor to bear in mind is whether your projected extension would put the price of your house far above that of all the others in the street. Where this would be the case, your best bet is to move, as you may not achieve this vastly higher price.

Another consideration is whether the projected extension would be out of keeping with the other houses in the street. A loft extension, for instance, might raise the roof in such a way as to make the place look like an eyesore. There is also the possible problem of being overlooked from, or looking into, neighbours' gardens or kitchens when you have a conservatory extension.

Loft extensions can put a burden on the foundations, so this is something to find out about before going ahead. A loft extension can also leave the house looking almost as cramped as before.

Although it is a pain to keep moving, not all 'improvements' are worth the fuss and bother, taking everything into consideration.

Creating space

Until about the 1970s, it never occurred to most of us that we could, instead of going through all the upheaval of moving, achieve our dreams by going through, admittedly, the almost as serious upheaval of extending our homes every which way – up, down, sideways, front and rear.

Everybody wants space – the more the better – and many houses have the potential to give us more room. Often it is possible to gain far more room than at first appears. Side and back extensions are usually the most popular and sensible ways in which to create extra space and, very often, they do not need planning permission. Outbuildings and summerhouses can also be converted into extra rooms or annexes to the main house.

Loft conversions are another good idea, so long as there is reasonable headroom, and basement conversions are also becoming increasingly popular where the construction of the house allows this. Garages can sometimes be turned into extra rooms and you may also be able to build on top of a garage at the side of a house to create an extra bedroom or bathroom.

Will planning permission be required?

All improvements that alter the structure and appearance of the property will need planning permission. It is sensible to contact your local council when you first have the idea to see whether or not permission is theoretically available. Never make any purchase or lifestyle change in advance of being granted planning permission as it's by no means certain.

If other houses in your street have already had loft or basement conversions done, then planning permission is often a formality. Converting a garage, however, may be more problematic, as many local authorities do not like garages to be reduced in number. It would, for instance, be impossible to get planning permission to create an extra room from a garage in a Notting Hill mews house, as parking is already pretty much impossible.

The value of experience

Before you even start along this road, bear in mind the wise words of Alexander Pope in his 'Essay on Man':

Be not the first by whom the new is tried

Nor yet the last to lay the old aside.

In my street, there are many back extensions. In fact, just about every house has one, but mine is the best, by far. Why? Because it is the latest, the newest! The next one undertaken in my street will be even better, as will each new extension because the builder or contractor learns more about what or what not to do. The moral of this is, whatever form of extension you are planning, do your homework and view finished examples of the kind of thing you have in mind, so that you can learn from other people's mistakes.

My extension has taken advantage of having an RSJ put in where the supporting wall was taken down, whereas earlier extensions incorporated the existing wall. Mine also has a glass roof, with glass strong enough to walk on, while earlier extensions had skylights. Mine connects to the main house, whereas earlier ones look more bolted on. What I'm saying is that, whatever type of extension or addition you want, it is worth waiting until the technology and know-how is well established in that area and all the early mistakes have been ironed out.

Extending outwards

What kinds of extensions are best?

If you have a typical Victorian terrace house with a dark, dank, unusable side return, then the best way to add light, space and value is with a ground-floor extension.

Mostly, side returns in their original state add little or nothing in terms of value or usable space to the house and are hardly more than a defect of the original design. Also, as they are at the back, extending into the space will not alter the look of the street at all. Victorian terrace houses in large cities usually have very small gardens at the back so it makes sense to turn this otherwise dead space into useful space rather than lose any of the garden.

Some houses lend themselves to extensions better than others, with the typical Victorian terrace being the easiest to extend. Whatever the design of your property, the look to avoid is the bolt-on – the best extensions appear to be integral to the house. The other thing is that, even when the extension is sensitively designed to blend in, it immediately gives the house a much more modern and contemporary look, which can make the rest of it seem old-fashioned by contrast. It is never easy to blend the old and the new in renovations, but more people prefer space to an absolutely authentic house with everything in character. After all, when they were built, they probably would not even have had bathrooms and electricity and nobody today can live without either. The worst look is the uPVC conservatory, which looks like an afterthought. Builder Michael Croft, who has undertaken many extensions, says, 'The important thing is to keep the character of the house when adding on. Planners usually want to know that you are avoiding the bolt-on look, which can take value away from the house. Nowadays, it seems that most people would prefer to stay where they are, so long as they can build on a decent extension.'

Planning permission

Normally you do not need planning permission for a single-storey extension or conservatory, provided you are not adding more than 15 per cent of the total volume of the existing property. Most extensions fall into the category of 'permitted development rights', unless the property is listed or in a conservation area.

If you have enough room, you may consider building an integral annexe on to the house. If the annexe being planned is a 'granny annexe', to be used by a dependant relative or maybe a teenager, planning permission is not required.

Converting outbuildings into separate dwellings, however, is another matter and not one to be entered into lightly as you are not allowed to create new, independent dwellings without planning permission. If the outbuilding is being converted to house an elderly relative, planning permission is not required, so long as the relative really is a dependant of the occupants of the main house. Building regulations, however, must be observed and an inspector from the council would need to make regular visits.

Is it worth it?

Make no mistake about it, extensions involve major work, requiring the full complement of builders and ancillary workers, plans, building regulations approval, a party wall agreement (possibly) and RSJs and Acrows, as well as the more or less complete disruption of your home.

Extensions generally take around three months, but can take longer, so, if you are renovating for profit, you have to take the cost and the time into account as well as the possible added value. If you will only, at a pinch, get your money back, an extension is probably not worth the time and trouble it involves. Leave it for the next person.

If it is your own home, there is no doubt that the extra quality of life an extension adds is enormous. To exchange a dark, cramped kitchen for a large, light and airy space just makes daily living so much better. A really huge kitchen with a massive dining table is, to my mind, the best present you could give to a house, give to yourself.

Colin and Sara's extension

An extension featured on 'my' Channel 4 property programme – *Room for Improvement* – cost over £90,000 and was architect-designed. Colin and Sara Lally – the young couple who commissioned the work – live in a four-bedroom terraced house in Fulham, south-west London. As with many terraced houses of its type, this house had a very small garden, which was overlooked by other houses all round. Therefore, privacy was going to have to be sacrificed.

The architect, Jenny Harborne, used glass to bring in as much light as possible, even though this would mean neighbours being able to see right in. The work took four months and cost more than double their original budget of £40,000. Because the house has no back entrance, all the building materials had to come through the house, creating dust and mess everywhere. Although having the extension means that they have lost about half of what was already a very small garden, this couple's view is that you don't buy this type of house for its garden anyway. Colin admits that he and Sara were scared stiff the whole time and reckon that employing an architect made the whole thing possible – they would never have been able to keep control of budget, builders, rubble, the work, building inspectors and so on otherwise. The work also required an engineer and surveyor.

Estate agents estimate that the extension has added around £100,000 to the value of the house, which cost £500,000 originally. However, as the extension cost over £90,000, it hasn't really added extra value – the couple would just about get their money back if they sold the house. It was expensive, but the Lallys reckon that they have gained because they now have an exciting, innovative extension that makes them the envy of their neighbours.

Some other points to consider

If you have room and can get planning permission, there is no doubt that the bigger you can make the kitchen, the better. When architect Richard Burton was designing his new house, he made the kitchen absolutely vast and with enough room to contain a gargantuan dining table, able to seat at least 20 people. He designed the house just for himself and his wife, but made the kitchen size an absolute priority. If only more architects would do the same!

When considering a back or side extension, first do your research. Look at others that have already been completed in your area, for your type of house, to get an idea of what the council has granted permission for already. If you happen to know a builder who specializes in extensions, ask to look at some of his work or, at the very least, see photos of the kind of work he does. This gets your eye in and enables you to hone your ideas. The really cheeky people pretend to be buyers and go round snooping in properties that they never intend to buy.

You also need to know how much, if any, value such an extension puts on the property. Often, it is not as much as you may imagine. It is always very difficult to add value with major work, as the work itself costs so much money. In any case, putting a figure on 'adding value' has to be an educated guess at best because the property market is subject to constant fluctuation. Also, elements beyond your control, such as a hike in the interest rates, a new road, new station, new airport or flight path, a big new estate, a shopping precinct, pedestrianization, parking facilities, schools and a whole host of other factors, can add or take away value whatever you do.

In my case, I added an extension to not so much increase the property's value, but so that it would not reduce in comparison with all the other houses in the row, which had extensions. Whatever monetary value the extension may or may not have added, the improvement it has made to my quality of life is incalculable. It has expanded my mind as well as my home.

The other main consideration with back and side extensions is how much, if any, of the garden you are going to lose and if it matters. Many Victorian terraces have tiny gardens that are not much use in any case, although I would always keep some outside space, for hanging out washing, putting plants or sitting outside on a sunny day. You can feel very boxed in if you have no outside space at all, but, having said that, glass roofs and conservatory-style extensions bring the outside in and the inside out. Big glass doors are a must, to open the house out into the outside space as much as possible.

Also, consider having the garden redesigned at the same time as you are planning the extension and have them done together, whenever the budget permits. Extensions create a phenomenal amount of mess, so, while the place is in upheaval generally, it makes sense to have the garden done at the same time and then it will fit in with the new scheme.

If you see something you wish to emulate, ask the owners who their builders or architects were and what they were like to work with, then, if there were no major problems, contact them to see if they can quote for your job.

Detailed architects' or other plans will need to be drawn up and submitted to the local planning department, even when planning permission is not required, as building regulations will need to be adhered to. A building inspector will make a number of visits to the site during the course of the work to check that none of the regulations are being infringed and issue a completion certificate when it has been finished. It is essential to have this completion certificate, especially when you come to sell the property.

If you are using an architect, the plans and design will cost around £4,000. I was lucky with my extension, because my builders had already done three in the same street. As they already had the plans, I did not need to have mine drawn up separately. You may be able to do the same if your planned extension is identical to another in your street. Very often, there is not a lot of choice with design, as you are constrained by space and the general dimensions of the house so another architect would come up with something very similar anyway.

Glass-roofed extensions enable you to see and be seen by next door if you are living in a typical terraced house, but there is not much you can do about this. From my extension, I can now see into next-door's bathroom. Similarly, they can now see right into my dining room extension from their back bedroom window. I considered having conservatory blinds, but realized that they would require as much rigging, ropes and operational skill as putting up the sails on the *Cutty Sark*, so I decided to sacrifice an element of privacy for the sake of not having the daily task of operating the blinds.

You do not need your neighbour's permission to build a back extension, but it is polite and neighbourly to keep them in the picture when undertaking work that will reduce their light, privacy and 'quiet enjoyment' of their home for some time. The vast upheaval involved in creating a back extension will intimately affect their lives as well. In my case, the garden wall was down for months as works progressed. It was only put back up at the very last stage. Note that if your extension requires the existing garden wall to be knocked down as mine did, you will need to have a party wall agreement in place before work can begin.

Loft conversions

In London, it costs at least £100,000 to buy a house with an extra room – and that's not counting the costs of buying, selling and moving. So, if you desperately need an extra room, it may be better to extend into the roof than have to go through the pain barrier that is moving house.

A Superior Climb – Time after Time

The most cost effective way of increasing space in a home is to make use of the loft. However, one of the most taxing problems is where to put the ladder or stairs. The decision usually involves sacrifices and "trade offs" in existing rooms.

Loft Centre Products offer one of the most comprehensive ranges of loft ladders, spacesaver stairs. Their technical department can generally offer options on how to get into the loft using the minimum amount of space. As specialists, Loft Centre Products are knowledgeable about the relevant Building Regulations and how they affect different types of stairs and spirals.

For more information on how Loft Centre Products can help you,
please contact us by either Tel: **01243 785246**, Fax: **01243 533184**
or e-mail **sales@loftcentreproducts.co.uk**

Is it possible?

The main thing to establish is whether or not a fully grown adult will be able to stand up in the space – or, more importantly, will be able to once the loft has been converted. You need to allow a head height of at least six foot six. I have viewed two loft conversions where the head height was only just over four feet, which puts the experience on a level with crawling around the lower decks of an eighteenth-century sailing ship.

Another time it might be worth considering a loft conversion is if you need a completely new roof anyway. New roofs require scaffolding and are a major job in themselves, so this might be the time to bite the bullet and go for the whole works in one hit.

Most Victorian and Edwardian houses lend themselves easily to loft conversions; Georgian houses may not as they often have tiny roofs and, in any case, are likely to be listed buildings. Many modern houses have roofs suitable for this type of conversion. Where the roof height is, or could be, made adequate in such cases, whether or not it can be done often hinges on how much valuable space the new staircase would take up. Bungalows, too, can often take loft conversions.

Water and electricity

After establishing that the roof is suitable, you need to assess whether or not there is power, plumbing, room and so on for an en suite. Personally, I would not consider going to the expense of a professional loft conversion unless you can squeeze in at least a basin and loo, if not a shower. The days when inhabitants of loft rooms were happy to go up and down stairs all the time to use the loo are over and you could find that, unless you do install a loo, the room will hardly be used, except as very expensive storage. In my view, a loo is more important than a shower, but is only feasible if the pipework allows it.

As far as a shower goes, the existing central heating system may not be up to the extra load another shower will put on it. If that is the case, a new, updated one will need to be fitted, which is a big expense in itself.

It may be the case anyway that the header tank, which is usually situated in the loft, has to move. A combi boiler, which does not need a header tank, may be the answer, but that could mean redoing your entire central heating system.

Planning permission and other consents

You will most probably need planning permission for a loft conversion. However, if other similar houses in the street have undergone these conversions, permission is usually easily obtained – provided you have the correct drawings and your neighbours have given permission.

Although planning permission for loft conversions may be a formality, there will almost certainly be restrictions on how the loft is to be converted. You may not be allowed to raise the existing roof height and have to build up at the back, with mansard windows, only Velux windows being permitted at the front.

Never be tempted to begin a loft conversion in advance of signing party wall agreements if the property is in a terrace or otherwise sharing a wall. This is necessary because the builder will almost certainly have to knock into next door's brickwork and, if this is done without a party wall agreement, neighbours can easily get an injunction to stop the work. You will have to pay for this agreement and the other party's surveyor. Ideally, there should be two different surveyors involved in preparing the agreement. A party wall agreement will certainly have to be in place when you come to sell, as it will be one of the documents you will be asked to produce as the sale proceeds.

If the floor has to be strengthened, which is usually the case, new beams will have to be fitted and building regulations come into play.

Insurance

Many loft conversions require scaffolding and, for this, your contractor must have public liability insurance. Specialist loft conversion firms will have all the necessary insurance and scaffolding arrangements in place, but it is always a good idea to make sure as you are the one ultimately responsible.

Where will the stairs go?

Loft conversions need to be designed carefully. Loft ladders are a nuisance if they have to be put up and down all the time, so the optimum solution to access is a solid staircase with a proper door at the top. Don't forget, however, that installing a proper staircase will inevitably take space away from the next floor down and may make the landing darker than before.

Who should draw up the plans?

Before making a final decision, contact several firms, as prices and ideas may vary. It may also pay you to have plans drawn up by an architect, although this is not always a foolproof approach. The advantage of having plans drawn up by an architect is that he or she is independent of the building company. If your plans are drawn up by the builder who will be carrying out the work, you are inevitably locked into that builder's methods of working and terms of payment permanently. It is not easy to extricate yourself if things start to go wrong.

How to pay for it

Although it is not usually recommended to pay anything in advance for building work, most loft conversion companies will ask for a deposit before work begins, as many expensive materials have to be bought. As with extensions, stage payments are usual, but do not pay until you are completely satisfied with each stage.

One piece of advice is to keep a large amount of money back for the final payment, as builders may not finish off a job completely if there is only a very small amount of money outstanding.

Practical considerations

Loft conversions, like all major renovation work, involve the making of a lot of mess. So, you need to know whether or not there will be a skip, who will take the rubbish away and how.

Peter Stedman, who runs The Loft Shop, which supplies all the necessary equipment for a DIY job (not amateur DIYers, however – at least 60 per cent of Stedman's sales are to builders), says that the two commonest mistakes made concerning loft conversions are:

∎   not having enough windows, so the loft is permanently dark;

∎   not getting the stairs right.

The wrong stairs act as an eternal reproach, as they are not easily rectified later.

Does a loft conversion add value?

Not necessarily. In my street, in West London, houses without loft conversions go for the same money as those with conversions. The reason for this is that the houses are small anyway, have no gardens to speak of and are really too claustrophobic for families. If you are not in the family market, loft conversions are commonly used as studies or offices or maybe as hobby rooms, such as to run a train set or Scalextric. They may, therefore, be considered an optional extra – nice if you've got one, but not something for which a buyer would be prepared to pay a premium.

Basement conversions

As technology improves, basement conversions are becoming increasingly popular – as kitchens, spare rooms, dens or teenagers' rooms. Of course, by no means all types of property are suitable for this type of conversion. You would need to have a cellar or basement already and some way of getting natural light into the new room. You would also certainly need planning permission.

Some practical considerations

Cellars were originally intended for storage and not as habitable rooms. As with loft conversions, there needs to be enough ceiling height already – or the possibility of excavating to achieve it – so that adults would not have to permanently stoop.

A major problem with basements is that, almost invariably, they are damp. It may not be possible for this to be completely eradicated, so you may have to settle for best results. Basements will almost certainly need tanking out, to address the damp problem, but this may not get rid of every scrap of damp.

Other considerations are the same as for loft conversions. For example, will you need a new staircase? What about heating? Is it possible to have a shower, loo and basin in the new basement? Again, the more facilities the new basement room has, the more it is likely to be used.

Many basements and cellars contain gas or electric meters, boilers and other unsightly accoutrements of modern living. Think about whether or not they will have to be re-sited and, if so, where?

Converting a basement into a flat

If you are considering creating a separate flat in the basement, then you will need planning permission and a separate heating and lighting system, plus separate meters. Ideally, basement flats should have their own front doors, but this is not possible with every conversion. Where a separate self-contained flat is created, there will be council tax issues and freehold/leasehold issues, too, especially if you are considering selling the basement flat as a separate entity.

Basement flats are never as popular or pricey as above-ground flats, although in areas that are generally highly desirable, they will still fetch a good price. So, if you are developing for profit, do thorough research into the prices of such properties to establish whether or not you really can add value with a basement conversion. In tall Victorian houses, the garden is often adjacent to the basement, so, if you convert the basement into a separate dwelling, you may lose the garden and, so, all your outside space.

Basement conversions that are autonomous add flexibility to your property and provide the possibility of an income should you want to rent it out. Alternatively, if the worst comes to the worst, you could live in the basement yourself and rent out the top of the house. If you can afford it, I would always advise anyone to develop an unused cellar or basement into a self-contained flat rather than just another room. It may take some time for any value to be added, if it is your own home, but, in densely populated areas where there is unlikely to be a significant increase in the housing stock, an extra place to live will always give your house the edge over others in the street without such conversions.

Garages

At one time, garages were considered to be very desirable and added significantly to the value of a house, particularly if they were integral. Times have changed and few people use garages for cars (unless they have classic, vintage or otherwise treasured or valuable cars) and, instead, think of them as storage and general junk rooms.

Is it possible?

First, check that you are actually allowed to convert the garage into an extra room. Where garages are integral, there may be strict limitations on what you are allowed to do with them. Many owners of small London mews houses with integral garages that they never use would love to be able to convert them into an extra room, but this is not allowed. Similarly, in some ex-local authority homes with integral garages, you are not allowed to convert them. This particularly applies with maisonettes where the tenure is leasehold and the lease governs what you can and can't do with the property. In both these cases, the fact that no alternative use can be made of the garage puts a definite ceiling on the selling price as most people would rather use the extra room as living space.

An exception must be made when a garage provides parking space where there would otherwise be none, such as in a city centre with double yellow lines as far as the eye can see. It would be total folly to convert a garage into a living area where there is otherwise nowhere to park. Never, ever do away with the only parking facility in the area for, although people will often pay a premium for an extra living room, they will pay much more of a premium to have parking space where this is difficult to obtain.

You may recall how earlier I gave the example of how, by creating two parking spaces in my Queen Anne listed house, I was able to double its value overnight and turn a property that previously was not that valuable into a highly coveted home. In this case, the house, having five floors, already had quite enough living space so there would have been nothing to gain, in any case, from turning those parking spaces into living accommodation.

In city areas, I have seen many small front gardens sacrificed to provide parking spaces, as this is considered to be the greater need. Where there are draconian restrictions on parking in the street, the provision of a parking space will add far more value than would an extra room. One carless neighbour of mine gets £100 a week from renting out the parking space in front of her house. She could command double that, if she wanted to.

If several owners of properties in your area have already converted garages into living spaces, ask to have a look to see how it's been done. Property experts advise that the 'converted garage' look is to be avoided, but this is not always easy. The clever way to convert a garage is to do it in such a way that nobody suspects there was once a garage there.

As with other conversions, even if you do not need actual planning permission, you will certainly need to comply with building regulations. Therefore, detailed drawings are required. Where planning permission is not required, the planners have no powers to make you alter your plans. Building regulations inspectors can, however, force you to comply with current regulations. As with other extensions, when converting a garage you will need a completion certificate.

If the garage is not integral, but attached to the house, you may consider building a bedroom or maybe another bathroom on top. As this will significantly alter the appearance of the property, you will need planning permission. In any case, you may also have to obtain permission for a change of use.

Where the garage is a separate entity and not required for cars, you may consider turning it into an annexe with en suite facilities and making it into a separate little house. If the annexe is considered to be a separate dwelling, it will, as with the self-contained basement conversion, have to have its own council tax banding. You may also need permission to create a separate dwelling and this may not be forthcoming.

Outbuildings and barns can often be converted into separate dwellings, but this is a major undertaking – almost on a par with building a new house. People often buy old manor houses and so on with outbuildings with a view to converting them into separate flats or houses that they will then sell or rent out, either on an assured shorthold tenancy or as holiday flats. This requires major negotiations with the local council and you could be in for a long haul.

The practicalities

Garages are most often found in newer properties and may provide the ideal solution to the problem of how to create extra space.

As with lofts and basements, garages are rooms not originally intended for human habitation and so may need a lot of work to upgrade them. There may not be insulation in the ceiling or cavity walls. You will need building regulations approval to bring the insulation up to modern standards and make the new space fit in with the rest of the property.

As with a basement, garages are likely to have damp problems. Consider how you will address this. Also, think about how you will heat the new room, as you may need a new central heating system if you are planning to have radiators. If you are thinking, for instance, of extending your dining room or kitchen into an integral garage, you may need the services of a structural engineer, as the house wall is almost certain to be load-bearing.

When converting former storage areas of your property into habitable rooms, always make sure that there will still be enough room left for storage. This is something developers (and architects) very often forget. I view countless conversions and renovations where there is not a single cupboard, nowhere to put so much as an ironing board or a suitcase, simply because every available space has been commandeered to make rooms bigger.

Although feng shui has encouraged us to clear our clutter, every household needs somewhere to store essential items, such as wellies, raincoats, umbrellas, Christmas trees and decorations, tools, garden stuff and archive material. Never add living space at the expense of taking away every last vestige of storage, as the first things potential buyers ask themselves are, 'Where am I going to put my bike?', 'Where do I put the camping gear?', 'Where do I store my books, CDs, magazines?', 'Where do I put my computer, filing cabinet, tax returns?' and so the list continues.

A home without adequate storage is unsaleable, however pretty and spacious it may look.

Does the addition add on value?

Many mortgage lenders have drawn attention to the fact that, increasingly, homeowners are deciding to stay put and extend rather than uproot and move. Mostly, additions are financed by remortgaging.

Before embarking on an expensive extension, however, it may be wise to consider whether or not it really will add value or whether your area is already overvalued, meaning that you may not even get your money back if you were to sell. In Wandsworth, south-west London – an area full of Victorian terraced houses and extension-mad owners – the difference in price between a house with a side return extension and one without is about £25,000 – the cost, in other words, of the extension.

Estate agents always advise homeowners to do what the market wants rather than follow their own desires as they may not make any money on resale – they may well lose money, in fact. Expert advice from estate agents to those considering adding on includes not overspending on very high-spec kitchens and bathrooms as, if the market slows, you may not be able to turn the wow factor into extra cash.

Beware of spending, too, in an area that is already overvalued as prices could come tumbling down. However, even if you do not plan to add on yourself, it may be worth obtaining outline planning permission, as you can then show buyers that the property has potential.

If the owner of the two-bedroom maisonette with a garage that I mentioned I was considering earlier had already obtained planning permission, I might well have bought the property. The fact that it had not been obtained indicated to me that, if I applied, I would be refused.

Whatever you do, make sure that any change is not too unusual or quirky for the average type of taste, as it could stay on the market for a long time, should you decide to sell.

Financing the addition

Mostly, additions are financed by remortgaging or obtaining a home improvement loan. There are now many kinds available and it is worth shopping around for the best deal.

Financial experts warn, however, that when remortgaging or obtaining finance for home improvements, you should not get yourself locked into a loan that is too much for you to afford the repayments or infinitely extend the term of the loan.

Many people go for interest-only mortgages, especially when financing renovations, but, by doing so, they may find that they never actually pay off the loan. Don't forget, either, that interest rates are always liable to fluctuation and another quarter per cent, for instance, on the loan may make repayments difficult.

The thing is never to finance improvements in the hope that property values will increase or you will get a rise at work. They may take a nosedive and you may be made redundant instead! Although in the past people often overstretched themselves with mortgages, and galloping inflation made this possible, the days of high inflation are over, at least for the time being.

Although everybody now wants wonderful homes, it must always be borne in mind that any loan you take out to achieve your goal has to be paid back with interest – and lenders never forget.

If you can pay cash and have done with it, then that is the ideal option. I would always pay cash where possible when improving my own home, rather than have money in the bank and borrow it at high rates of interest. There is no sense in locking yourself into unpayable debt. If you look around, you will find that there are quite a few more options than was the case just a few years ago that will mean you can turn your vision into reality.

Renovation insurance

It is possible to obtain special renovation insurance for your project. Ordinary household policies will not cover you for repairs, alterations or maintenance work, or if the property is unoccupied for more than 30 days. In most cases, renovation insurance is not a legal requirement, and usually builders, scaffolders and other contractors will have their own insurance anyway. Scaffolders must, by law, have liability insurance.

Renovation insurance covers accidental damage, damage by fire, theft of materials and other hazards. As with all insurance policies, only you can decide whether it is worth it, but it is certainly advised where you are not there yourself or are living in another part of the country, where there are expensive materials lying around or where the renovation itself is very expensive.

Some mortgages and home improvement loans may require such insurance.

Windows

The appearance and design of windows are becoming ever more important, as discerning renovators nowadays steer clear of ghastly plastic and metal windows and are returning to wood. It is not always possible, of course, to install wooden windows and, if you live in a block of flats, your windows will have to conform exactly to the design of all the others.

Although plastic windows are undoubtedly much cheaper than wooden ones to install, the belief that they are maintenance-free is untrue. The plastic biodegrades in time, and most plastic windows have a life of about 20 years before they have to be replaced. By contrast, timber windows last more or less for ever and can be painted and repaired more or less indefinitely. It is not unusual for timber windows to last a hundred years or more.

Plastic windows warp and discolour over time and allow for condensation between panes. It may not be possible to get rid of this condensation. Original wooden windows are made from seasoned wood, and the modern ones are as energy-efficient as uPVC.

If you have a listed building, you will most probably not be allowed to put in plastic windows but must install wooden windows of the type originally there. And don't forget that this can be enforced.

Energy efficiency

Energy efficiency is increasingly becoming a selling point for houses, and it is likely that in the near future all homes put up for sale will require an energy efficiency rating, just like those found on cookers and fridges. An energy performance certificate was going to be a compulsory aspect of the Home Information Pack that is due to be introduced in 2007, but this was scuppered at the last minute by Housing Minister Ruth Kelly. Now, home condition reports are voluntary, and sales will not depend on them.

However, energy efficiency for homes can now be graded on a scale of A to G, with A being rated the most efficient. There will actually be two separate ratings: one for energy efficiency and the other for the impact of the property's CO_2 emissions on the environment.

Thus, an A-rated home will have a solar-heated water system, low-energy light bulbs, state-of-the-art thermostatic controls, ultra-high-efficiency boilers, triple-glazed windows with a heat-reflecting window coating, 10-inch-thick loft insulation and wind turbines. Very few homes will have all these features, at least for many years, but these are the aspects to aim for.

A G-rated house, by contrast, will be terraced and have wooden floors, draughty windows, no loft insulation, cavity windows, an old, inefficient boiler, a low energy-rated washing machine and old thermostats.

These ratings are for information only and do not necessarily affect the saleability of a house. The Energy Saving Trust (www.est.org.uk) has tips on how to make your home more energy-efficient, with information on how much value each energy-saving device is likely to add to your property.

About Smart Systems

The progress of technology has seen many advances in the home automation market, and more and more people are applying this science to their own homes.

These systems allow the user to experience home cinema at its very best, intelligent lighting schemes, multi-room audio distribution and touch pad remote control over all sections of a smart system.

The data installation caters for all SKY, DVD, Ethernet and telephone distribution.

By using these systems, you are achieving a very high standard of home automation and will enjoy the seamless way it integrates with your life.

There are varied levels of smart system control on the market to suit all projects and budget and are best understood by discussing your options with one of our experienced team.

About us

At HTL we bring together all of the necessary aspects of the smart system detailed above, and by using an experienced project engineer to oversee the contract we can provide a smooth, stress free installation.

The engineer can give advice, programme of works and will assist with any queries the client may have.

We are a medium sized company based in the South West and work on many variously sized projects from private dwellings to large multi property developments; we are accustomed with working alongside developers, architects and interior designers. We also hold NICEIC registration and can therefore offer a complete package.

About your project

If you think that we could be of some service to you then please call or email us to make an appointment, alternatively view our website and download a colour brochure.

www.htl-smartsystems.co.uk

Case studies

Dart Marina (Dartmouth)

This contract consisted of forty five luxury apartments situated in the marina at Dartmouth, South Devon.

The project ran from Summer 2004 to Summer 2006 and was a milestone for smart systems in the South West.

This development exceeded the home automation standard by offering Lutron controlled lighting systems, multi-room audio schemes, plasma and surround sound technology.

This contract had at times eighteen of our skilled team to make sure the project handed over on time, and with the highest standard finish.

These properties were cabled for a complete system but had only a section of the capabilities possible; this meant the developer could produce smart home technology whilst offsetting some costs to the end user who would purchase the optional extras directly with us.

South Sands Hotel (Salcombe)

This development ran from Spring 2004 to the Spring of 2006 and is situated in a breathtaking beach landscape and is now a smart enabled hotel/restaurant; this project transformed an aged hotel and produced eight luxurious apartments with sea view no more than 20m away. It also boasts twelve, five star hotel suites each with their own lighting mood scenes, large plasma's and bathroom televisions. These units are situated on top of one of Salcombe's finest restaurants which have a 60in. plasma, audio system and mood scenes to create that eating experience.

The Monastery (Woodleigh)

This hundred year old monastery was styled with great care encapsulating the old with the new; the project started in the Winter 2005 and is still ongoing. Once complete, the monastery will house eight state of the art and up to date apartments each of which have access to their private gym, pool and tennis courts. A simple text message from your mobile phone can activate the heating systems to warm to a set temperature for your arrival. A security alarm system is installed with the capability of having "red care" (police monitored lines) installed if required.

+(44) 845 021 2000

6 Renovations and restorations

Many people have a dream of buying an old wreck and lovingly restoring it to its former glory. The television series *Restoration* has done much to encourage people to think about buying dilapidated or abandoned homes and breathe new life back into them.

Make no mistake, however, restoration is an expensive and difficult process and there may be many moments of despair before you can enjoy the final result. Indeed, with a really major restoration, the work may never be finally completed. When you come to sell, you may not even get your money back, let alone make a profit.

This said, you will have the inestimable pleasure of living in something really beautiful and, with a lovely old house, nothing can ever truly ruin it. To me, a very beautiful old house is like a beautiful actress; increasing years may add wrinkles and decrepitude, but nothing can completely destroy the original charm and appeal.

If you are interested in doing a major renovation, the quality you need more than any other is imagination. You need to be able to envisage what the finished result will look like. It also helps to have some idea of what you want to achieve with a dilapidated building, whether it is restoring it to how it was before or adding on extensions, roof rooms, conservatories and so on to increase its size.

The ideal restoration is one that preserves as many of the original features as possible, while making it a comfortable place to live in. Most people want modern bathrooms, power showers, central heating and up-to-date kitchens, whatever the place may have been like originally.

It is also a good idea to make your home as maintenance-free as possible. Although wooden windows look far nicer than uPVC, they are not always the best option. I personally do not like uPVC, but, in some cases, it may simply not be practical or feasible to restore the original wooden windows. For absolute purists, uPVC windows are on a par with nodding dogs and fluffy dice in car windows – something nobody with any aesthetic sense would tolerate for a moment. However, in situations where the weather or construction conditions make restoration that is close to the original impossible, then compromises have to be made. At the back of my South Coast flat, in a listed building, I have sneaked in a uPVC window as the original window had long been lost anyway and the resulting contraption a total nightmare. Also, in conditions where the weather would mean yearly maintenance bills, some modern uPVC windows may be more practical, even if they are not in absolute keeping with the style of the rest of the building.

There are companies that make uPVC sash windows that blend in very closely with the originals, yet do not need painting or much other maintenance. In some situations, it may be worth swallowing your pride for ease of fitting and aftercare.

Traditional flooring may also take a lot of looking after. Few people want to spend all their spare time cleaning floors. Tiled floors look nice in old properties, but they can be extremely cold underfoot and may also look forbidding.

I used to be much more concerned about using natural materials than I am now. This is partly because I came to the realization that, in the past, natural materials were often used solely because that was all there was available then, whereas now, other options abound and it's not necessarily a bad thing to use something else. What must be avoided, always, is taking away any original character from the property. However, the reality is that, in most cases, old or dilapidated buildings will have already had much of their character removed by previous owners.

It is not uncommon, for instance, for Georgian houses to have been desecrated by having 1950s tiled fireplaces installed, all the original panelling removed or all the original cornicing taken away. In such cases, when you 'restore', you are, in effect, bringing in a modern or 'fake' version of the original.

What you do need to bring to any sensitive restoration is an aesthetic sense of what will look good, whether it is absolutely authentic or not.

The right builders

Although jobbing handymen may be able to fit kitchens and bathrooms and, at a pinch, maybe erect a passable extension, where complete renovation or restoration is required you really do need good builders. This probably means a well-established local firm with craftsmen who are used to this type of work.

Marianne Suhr, who co-presented the *Restoration* television series, believes that most ordinary modern builders do not understand old houses. She says, 'If it doesn't come prefabricated, your average builder is out of his depth.' Builders, she believes, have, in the main, lost touch with the processes of traditional building and we are killing old buildings by covering them with cement.

These days, she says, the craze is for everything to be smooth and perfect, even when walls and ceilings are rough and not exactly at right angles to each other, as is almost always the case in old houses: 'The beauty in older houses lies in their imperfections and differences in texture. I'm not saying that we have to live as people did when the house was built — you have to have modern bathrooms, plumbing and electricals.' However, the fabric of the house, she believes, has to be restored in as traditional a way as possible.

So, before even considering buying a completely dilapidated building, it would be sensible to research the available builders in the area, see if they understand old bricks, old roofs, old materials and traditional crafts. There is also the point that builders who are this knowledgeable are, very likely, going to be much more expensive than the average kind. If you need a project manager, this will also add to the cost.

Most people who have successfully renovated properties advise using local builders. This is because they generally take care over their work as they need to preserve their good reputation in the neighbourhood. Local contractors are also likely to be acquainted with the planning and environmental departments of the local council and can advise on the best ways in which to gain permission, where this is indicated.

Planning permission

If the building is listed, you have no other choice as there will be strict regulations on what you are and are not allowed to do to the façade and there may even be restrictions on how much you can alter the interior, too. Also, if any aspect of the building is mentioned in the Land Registry entry, you may need permission in order to alter or adapt it. For instance, I needed planning permission to knock down a tiny, windowless room in my Grade II-listed flat as it was on the plans when they were drawn up in the 1940s, when the original hotel was turned into flats. Equally, if you want to knock down a supporting wall in a listed building, you will need planning permission before you can do so. You would also need permission to put in new windows or make the existing windows bigger or smaller.

Even when granted, planning permission does not last forever. If you do not start work within five years, you will have to reapply – and this time permission may be refused.

Developing for profit?

If you are planning to restore an old house, there is probably not much sense in 'thinking like a developer', as TV presenter Sarah Beeny puts it. The average developer, with a beady eye on a quick profit, would instantly see that there is no money to be made from lovingly restoring an old, heritage or listed building in the way it should be done. Traditional materials may not be available from edge-of-town DIY stores and not many developers would want to put back a lath and plaster ceiling. Instead, they would want to use modern plasterboard. Developers have to think of quick tricks and cheap ways round problems to maximize their profit, while still complying with building regulations, of course.

Marion Mathews and Renske Mann, who, you may recall from earlier, are restoring a 200-year-old cottage overlooking the sea in north Devon, are trying to preserve as much as possible of the original look. At the same time, they need a modern kitchen, modern heating, en suite bathrooms and big windows. The original cottage had only one very small window on the seafront, through which very little could be seen. The whole point, for them, of buying the cottage is to have the wonderful view of the harbour, but it can only be enjoyed from much bigger windows than the original property possesses. With this location, the local council is concerned to preserve the heritage look of the place, which means that uPVC windows are out. These kinds of costs could simply not be considered if they were simply carrying out the work to make a profit as it would be quickly eaten away by such items.

Finding and financing the right place

Finance is often a problem with restoration, as costs can easily run away with you. Marion and Renske are paying for their cottage purchase and renovation with a 10-year mortgage. The money for the repayments is coming from the rent they receive from their buy-to-let apartment in London. It was a piece of luck that Renske's employers suddenly started paying her a lot more money to do a lot more work just at the moment when they needed every penny they could lay their hands on. However, I do believe that, when a project is right, somehow the money will be found (there is more on this subject later in this chapter).

Some examples of people who have succeeded

Finding the right project in the first place requires a combination of logical, rational thinking and intuition. For instance, Marion and Renske believe that it is extremely important to have compatible people in the area as friends. As it has turned out, several of their friends have already bought little cottages in the same street in the same little town, so already they have the beginnings of a happy social life. It can be a mistake to buy somewhere on impulse and then discover that it actually does not meet any of your day-to-day living and social requirements.

Helen and Arthur Franks, a writer and engineer, respectively, recently finished work on a 1930s bungalow in Steyning, West Sussex, which they bought as a second home and bolthole for themselves, their children and grandchildren. The original tiny, two-bedroom bungalow needed major work and had been sitting on the market unsold for a long time because of this. Helen and Arthur decided to expand the property into a four-bedroom, two-bathroom home that would be big enough for their children and grandchildren to use.

They are naturally inclined towards heritage-type houses, so why did they choose a dismal-looking bungalow in the first place? Helen said:

We didn't choose a bungalow as such, it was the location that appealed. The bungalow is in an area of outstanding natural beauty and what we wanted most of all was a view. Then we wanted to be in a small town, not on a main road, and within easy driving distance from our main house in London.

We had previously had a weekend home in Brighton, but Brighton, shall we say, got too young for us. Also, it was difficult to park and there was no view.

In an ideal world, we would have preferred a Grade II-listed building to a tacky bungalow, but we couldn't afford the kind of thing we would have liked and would have had to settle for somewhere on the main road with no parking and no view. So, we decided to go for the bungalow, and remodel it to our design.

First of all, an architect drew up plans, then they researched the builder situation until they found a local firm in Steyning:

We let the neighbours know what we were doing and showed them our plans. Because we communicated with them at every turn, none of them objected and, as the drawings were very detailed and we were using local firms, there was no problem with planning permission. It was a very big and expensive undertaking and it has all worked out exactly as we wanted.

The bungalow, situated on a large, end plot, now has a huge extension encompassing large kitchen, dining area and living area – all separate entities, yet connected. The main bedroom has an en suite and there is a second bathroom for the other three bedrooms.

Helen believes that there are two main secrets to success when undertaking major renovation or rebuilding. First, employ an extremely reputable firm of local builders. Second, make sure that the lines of communication are kept open all the time. She says:

> It's very useful to be able to pick up the phone when builders are at a loss and think something is beyond them. In the main, it's better to go with what you know that they can do.
>
> If your builders intimate that they can't do something you set your heart on, you must be prepared to change your mind or compromise. You have to listen to your builders as some things might not be possible and one thing that you are employing them for is their expertise.
>
> Ours was a big, complicated job and, because we were not there ourselves all the time, we needed a project manager who could be permanently on site. Even so, it was an exhausting and stress-making enterprise, but definitely worth it!

The Franks decided to go for a cheap, rather than luxury, look inside and bought much of what they needed from Ikea. Helen says:

> You have to go for an appropriate look. The bungalow could never be grand and, although we did not renovate it for profit, we wanted an informal, easy look. For instance, we went for a B&Q laminate floor rather than quarry tiles. Apart from the laminate being very much cheaper, our builders told us that, if we had a tiled floor, it would take at least a day for the tiles to heat up in the winter. For most of the weekend, they would be freezing cold underfoot. This is the kind of thing you have to think about – and listen to your builders.

Although they have used cheap Ikea kitchen units and bought cheap furniture, the place does not look cheap because it is so very well designed and colour coordinated. Helen says that you have to like going to Ikea (or similar) and be prepared to spend time matching colour and fabric samples to get a streamlined look. Helen and Arthur have also gone for uPVC, rather than wood, but have kept the original 1930s doors throughout.

Their new neighbours are amazed at what they have achieved, which has had the effect of 'glamourizing' the enclave where they bought their property and enhancing the general value of the area.

Helen says, 'It was almost a complete rebuild, but we would not have been allowed to raise the roof, for instance, although we could possibly have had a loft room.' However, extra light floods into the kitchen and dining room as a result of clever use of skylights.

Now that the bungalow is finished, Helen says that she likes everything being on one floor: 'In London, our house is on three floors, which means we are always going up and down stairs. Our house in Brighton was also on three floors, so for us it is a luxury not to have any stairs.'

The Franks did not buy their bungalow as an investment and reckon that they spent over £300,000 on the purchase and renovation. However, because the renovation is so special and in a highly desirable area, they would always at least get their money back if they decided to sell. They used money from the sale of their Brighton home to finance the purchase and renovation.

Listed building consent

Many heritage-type houses are listed and, as I know from experience, this is both a curse and a blessing. The blessing is that they cannot be desecrated by people putting in uPVC windows and doors and bolt-on extensions, but the curse is that they can be so difficult and expensive to restore that they are often just allowed to rot.

Although local councils have draconian powers to make you restore a listed building to its original state rather than make lots of unsympathetic changes, no council in the world can force you to carry out repairs unless they are willing to foot the bill and, naturally enough, they are not. In some cases, though, small grants may be available, which are paid in arrears, once the work has been completed to the council's satisfaction.

One particular listed building – Embassy Court on Brighton's seafront – was once a fine, art deco apartment block. Over the years, it deteriorated until eventually it looked like the kind of bombed-out building you might find in Beirut. In fact, the block was known locally as 'Beirut'. It was the most terrible eyesore, but nobody did anything about it. Eventually, after the apartment block had been crumbling and decaying for about 20 years, work began on restoration.

It's the same story all over the country. The listed house I bought in Richmond had trees growing in the living room and was inhabited by squatters who had turned it into a warren of seedy bedsits. Yet, bad as it was, no work could be done until listed building consent was in place – and that took two years to obtain. This applies to the inside arrangements as well as the outside appearance.

Never imagine that you can start work on a listed building *before* the consents are in place, as this is a criminal offence. Councils can – and do – order people to dismantle or otherwise remove improvements if these are not to their liking.

If a building is 'listed', this means that it has been designated by the Department of Culture, Media and Sport as of historic or architectural interest and this is why controls on what you can do to it are tight. You would be best to discuss your renovation plans with the conservation officer of the relevant local authority before buying, but, if not then, certainly before proceeding with any works, for the reasons given above.

Don't forget that, regardless of what the council thinks, whenever planning applications are sent round to the neighbourhood and posted in public areas, your neighbours may well object to what you intend to do. Whenever planning any major restoration or renovation, it is always worth keeping on good terms with neighbours, as they have greater powers to destroy all your fine plans than you might imagine. In extreme cases (as we shall see in the next chapter), neighbours may decide to get up a petition to prevent you building or restoring.

Conservation areas

If the building is not listed but in a conservation area, the controls are less stringent but still mean that you can't just do whatever you like. You would be allowed to extend the house by 10 to 15 per cent without obtaining planning consent, so long as the extension is not at the front and would not adversely affect the street scene. Renovation magazines often have a big section on 'permitted development', which covers renovations that have not transgressed any of the set limits. The reason for these sections being big is that permitted development is a highly complicated subject with its own arcane rules and regulations. If the extension you are planning in a conservation area is larger than that permitted, you will then need to gain planning permission. In any case, it is advisable to send a drawing of your proposals to the planning department of the local council to confirm whether or not your planned changes fall within the terms of permitted development.

Some conservation areas have been issued with an 'Article 4 Direction', which takes away all the permitted development rights. The best advice, as ever, is not to leave anything to chance where expensive refurbishments are being considered.

Noise and noise prevention

When considering a major renovation or restoration, it is important to pay close attention to noise abatement. If you are changing the use of the property or part of it, you will of course have to abide by the stringent noise-reducing regulations now in place. Even if you are not required to put in sound insulation by law, it is certainly worth doing, simply to make life more bearable and enjoyable.

In Victorian times, heavy curtains and thick carpets ensured a reasonable degree of sound insulation from one floor to another. However, the modern love affair with wooden, laminate or tiled floors and the tendency to put up blinds instead of heavy curtains mean that noise ricochets round buildings in a way that it didn't really do in the past. That, plus the amplified sound coming from hi-fi systems and TV sets, with or without home cinema speakers, means that noise has become a major problem, especially in flats.

The latest Part E building regulation revisions relating to noise and sound came into effect in January 2004 and apply to new buildings, conversions and changes of use. Builders will now have to prove to the satisfaction of a building control officer that construction meets the requirements of the building regulations and they may be subject to mandatory testing.

Walls and floors in every residential conversion, new build and extension project are affected by these revisions. The only exceptions are refurbishment projects in listed residential buildings where there will be a 'test and declare' option if the new standards cannot be achieved.

The regulations are, of course, extremely technical, but it is advisable to contact the relevant building control body for guidance on new floor and wall construction.

Money matters

Unless you are a cash buyer and also have plenty of cash for the restoration, it is not easy to raise the money to buy an uninhabitable property or one that needs major work. Most mainstream lenders are understandably wary of such projects, fearing that the buyer will default on the mortgage, leaving a half-finished and unsaleable property. Therefore, it is seen as too great a risk for them.

If you are trying to get on to the property ladder, it would probably be unwise for you to look for somewhere that needs major renovation. Mortgage lenders prefer to advance money for properties that are already habitable and in good condition. The worse the condition, the more money you have to have in the bank before undertaking such work. Even though dilapidated properties tend to be cheaper to buy than those in good condition, they are not seen as such a good bet from the lender's point of view. Indeed, one of the reasons for them being cheap is that it is difficult to get a mortgage on them.

It is not completely impossible to borrow money for this type of conversion, but the deal is not as good as for an ordinary mortgage. The Norwich and Peterborough Building Society, for instance, offers a 'brown mortgage' especially for conversions and restorations. It will lend up to 85 per cent of the current valuation or purchase price, which means that you would have to put down a 15 per cent deposit at least.

Then, money for the renovation work is released in a series of staged payments as each phase of work is completed and once a valuer has inspected the site. Because the payments are made in arrears, you need sufficient capital to fund at least the initial stage of the work.

The Norwich and Peterborough Building Society also provides detailed guidance and advice on how you should get the work done. The first phase is, naturally, the major structural work, such as the replacement of floors, walls and ceilings, damp courses and electrical work. When this has been done and inspected, the Norwich and Peterborough Building Society will release 50 per cent of the remaining mortgage funds.

A further 25 per cent of funds will be released after the second phase has been completed. This includes the installation of kitchen and bathroom, plastering and flooring. Once the conversion has been completed, with all the decorating done, the final 25 per cent of funds is released. The monthly mortgage payments go up as each staged payment is released.

The Ecology Building Society specializes in providing mortgages that 'give an ecological payback'. This includes those for dilapidated properties in need of renovation and non-domestic properties, such as barns, that can be converted into homes. The society will lend up to 90 per cent of the purchase price of the property, plus up to 90 per cent of renovation costs, so borrowers need at least a 10 per cent deposit and enough capital to carry out the first stage of the work.

Buildstore is a specialist company catering for self-builders and home renovators. If you are approved for its Accelerator mortgage, it will lend up to 95 per cent of the property price or value, plus up to 95 per cent of the renovation costs. Buildstore also gives out the money in staged payments, but this time in advance rather than in arrears, as with the other two building societies. This means that borrowers have the money to hand to pay for materials and labour, so those with less capital may still be able to proceed with a renovation. With this company, you have to buy a valuation guarantee policy, costing around £200.

Although mortgage lenders may appear to be falling over themselves to shove money at you, it is important to remember that they are commercial institutions intent on making money out of you and that is their main aim, however the deal is dressed up. With this in mind, figures have to be worked out very carefully indeed. Where money is short, as it usually is, you have to try for as many fixed prices as possible so that things don't spiral out of control.

The process

Those of us who have restored horrible old wrecks and now have beautiful homes know just how satisfying it can be. In my time, I have restored and renovated six very tired, dated properties and, although all have shown a profit, this was not the motivating factor for undertaking the work. I liked being able to put my own stamp on the place, individualize it and customize it.

A few years after I sold my Queen Anne house in Richmond, built in 1688, I went back to have a look at it. I was astonished at how beautiful it now looked. There was a hand-built kitchen in place of the collapsing units I had inherited and a wonderful dining room next door. Two en suite bathrooms had been added and the whole place had the look of a rock star's mansion. Indeed, it sold for a rock star price and is now worth at least £1.7 million. I was not there to see it restored to its full glory myself, but it was satisfying to have had a hand in the process.

Although such moments of pride and enjoyment are exhilarating, do not be lulled into thinking that restoration is anything other than incredibly time-consuming, expensive and has its moments of extreme trauma and frustration. Our two sons, looking back, say that they vividly remember my ex-husband and myself sitting at the kitchen table poring over endless documents from the local council and covering our heads with our hands in our extreme despair as we were getting nowhere. Then, just as we thought we had got over the worst, our next door neighbour called to say that sewage from our house was seeping all over her garden. We thought she must be mad, but went to have a look and she was right. That was another huge bill of thousands of pounds. So it goes on. Expect the unexpected when restoring, as you will certainly get it. You will find as you go on that your house does all kinds of spiteful things to you. Just make sure that you have the stamina to cope.

Many people have said to me that it all becomes much easier if there are two of you to laugh with each other when things go wrong and take some of the strain. I would agree – restoration is an extremely lonely process when you are on your own. However, if you are working with a partner, you must be in agreement about what you want – you don't want to add domestic or marital arguments to the ones you may already be stacking up with planners, workmen and neighbours.

Conversions

If you are considering turning a house into a number of flats or, conversely, creating a single-occupancy home from a house divided into several units, you will need to register a change of use. When you do this, extremely strict building regulations come into force.

If you are thinking of creating several units from a previous single-occupancy house, you must first obtain planning permission to do this. Detailed plans will have to be drawn up and submitted to the appropriate council department. Then you have to wait to see whether or not they will be approved. In the meantime, neighbours will be informed and asked to either give their consent or object to your plans. If they object, it could either take a long time to get planning permission through or it could be turned down. At the very least, any objections from neighbours will hold up permission being granted.

When undertaking conversions, fire safety and sound-proofing regulations will have to be abided by – and these are very expensive. With some conversions, you may have to have a fire escape at the back; at the very least, the fire precautions must be approved.

In recent years, as we saw earlier, sound-proofing has become a major issue. When Nicola and Matthew Naish converted a five-bedroom house in Worthing into five flats, they had to put at least a 30 cm (12 in) thick layer of sound-proofing material between each floor, which lowered the ceilings and meant that the original cornicing was hidden. The cost of this was also extremely high. As they were property developing, they had to make sure that, if they built in all the elements that they were required by law to include, the project would still give them a profit. Their situation was made worse by the fact that the area had only just been declared a conservation area. They were, in fact, the first developers to be hampered by the new rules and regulations. Despite the aggravation, the result was that they achieved a lovely conversion where every flat was snapped up the minute it came on to the market, at the full asking price. The downside was that the development cost about twice the expected amount, but they still made a profit on it.

Increasingly, people are converting commercial or industrial premises into homes. Examples include post offices, schools, churches, former pubs, warehouses, factories, fire stations and police stations.

If you like the prospect of doing something like this, the first thing you need to do once you have found an appropriate building is obtain permission for a change of use from the local council. Estate agents warn that this can take a long time – up to two years is not uncommon, even when the former commercial premises have been boarded up for years. If you do not apply for change of use consent, though, the council could order you to stop work at once.

In some cases, the local authority will order a developer to retain some of the existing structure so as not to spoil the look of the street. In the case of a former pub or shop in a village being converted for residential use, you may need to retain original signs, front doors and other features. You may also be required to call the residence 'The Old Post Office', 'The Old Pumping Station' or whatever.

Most estate agents believe that conversions of former non-residential premises are best left to the professionals as the process of getting permission is so complicated that it deters the average amateur developer.

Whatever you do, never be tempted to buy a charming former post office, water mill or warehouse before all permissions are in place and plans drawn up. Before even making an offer or considering such a purchase, I would pay an architect, builder or surveyor to give the place the once-over and let you know approximately how much the work would be likely to cost and which features you would be able to add or take away. Otherwise, you could be left with something that turns out to be a very expensive mistake.

7 Self-build

Would you like to live in a cramped caravan in a cold, open field while you construct your very own house?

This is very often what you have to be prepared to do to achieve the dream of living in a home that you have designed and built yourself. However, in spite of the privations often suffered during construction, not to mention steadily mounting costs, self-build is becoming an ever more popular option, with a growing number of magazines and yearly exhibitions aimed at this fast-expanding market.

Many experts believe that it is often actually cheaper to build your own house from scratch than to buy a wreck and then restore it. At least with your own house, you are getting exactly what you want – well, so long as you operate within planning constraints, and self-builders warn that these restrictions can be extremely tight indeed. It is not unknown for council inspectors to order self-builders to replace their specially made doors because they are deemed too small to meet current regulations and then make them spoil the entire look of the thing by insisting on ramps for wheelchair access when a disabled person would never want to live there because the rest of the house would be totally impractical for them.

Michael Jordan's experience

Michael Jordan has so far self-built four houses. I went to see him in his latest and very splendid home near Bideford in Devon. The house, a massive chalet-style construction, has a huge kitchen, separate dining room, living room and study downstairs, plus four bedrooms, all with en suite facilities, upstairs. There is also a double garage with a guest suite above it. The house, down a secluded lane, took nearly two years to build and cost a total of around £350,000. Mike, a retired local government official, did much of the work himself.

How did it all start?

Mike, who now lives in the house in Devon with his wife, Tricia, and two adult daughters, Claire and Rebecca, said that, in the beginning, the main consideration was money:

> Going back about 20 years, we were living in a little terrace house in Surrey and couldn't afford to move up the property ladder. Then, I was offered a job in Devon and decided to take it. Here, property was cheaper and we managed to swap the Farnborough house for a detached chalet bungalow. We got more for our money, but realized that, if we wanted to make money from property, we had to start developing ourselves.

Financing the build

Mike and Tricia bought a dilapidated house to do up in nearby Torrington for £9,500, then sold their main house to buy a plot to start building their own:

> In those days, you had to say you wanted the money for improvements to your own home to get the finance. You could not get specialist self-build mortgages, as you can today.
>
> So, we sold the main house and moved to the little Torrington terrace, where we lived until we could find the ideal plot to start building. We found the right piece of land, which was going at auction for a sealed bid. I had no idea how much the plot would fetch, so I came up with a figure of £25,000. At the time, this sum was a record for North Devon, but we got it. It was a nice plot, with an acre of land, overlooking the estuary.
>
> I had planning permission for a five-bedroom house and spent every spare hour in the evenings and weekends working on it.

How to know what to do and a handy tip

Mike had learnt building construction on a course at Guildford College and, although he never became a builder full time, had always loved building. 'I get a kick out of it,' he says. 'We did as much as possible ourselves, with Tricia doing the tiling. We did employ contractors and specialists, although I did the project managing myself.'

Mike feels that the secret of making self-build pay is to create a close rapport with builders' merchants:

If an ordinary person goes to a builders' merchants, he will pay the full price for materials, but if you have an account there, you can get up to 40 per cent off. For instance, if you bought a breeze block, it would cost you 75p plus VAT, but if you bought a batch, the blocks would cost 35p each. You definitely have to bargain and you get an extra discount if you buy in bulk.

The builder won't pass on that discount, but, rather, the reverse – he will add on a 5 to 7 per cent handling charge. So, by employing builders, you actually pay more for materials. After a time you get to know how much things cost.

The next step

Not long after Mike finished this house, he worried that he might be made redundant and sold it. The family then moved to Barnstaple and took stock of their position. In the event, Mike was not made redundant, but spent around seven years trying to find another plot:

We knew exactly what we wanted. We did not want sea views as the salt water and constant wind from the sea makes all the windows salt up and the tiles rattle, but what we did want was a garden and privacy, plus loads of trees.

Eventually, we found this plot after seeing a lot of over-priced places. Nowadays, it's not so easy to find the right plot as everybody wants to try self-build and the prices are shooting up all the time. There are, for instance, no plots round here at all at the moment. Also, you are totally governed by the planning department, especially as nowadays all plots of any size have to have a certain amount of affordable housing on them.

The concept of 'affordable' housing is creating a distinct nimby (not in my back yard) attitude among self-builders and small-time developers, as well as the neighbours already in the area. Rightly or wrongly, the fear is that affordable housing – although aimed at key workers who would not otherwise be able to afford housing in the area – would actually attract different, undesirable types of people, creating all kinds of problems. Very many modern developments now include an area of affordable housing and the results are mixed.

The problem with planning permission

Mike and Tricia's present plot cost £160,000 and planning permission had already been granted for a three-bedroom bungalow:

> This was not what we wanted, so we spent a lot of time trying to design another bungalow. That didn't work because the neighbours objected, saying that their privacy would be adversely affected.
>
> Things got so bad that the neighbour next door did a leaflet drop saying that she didn't want this new house built and she got up a petition, the effect of which was that our first planning application was rejected. The planning department said it was too big and not in keeping with the rest of the houses. Also, I had put in for a triple garage and that was rejected as well on the grounds that there was no way anybody should be allowed to have three garages.

Mike says that his job at the local council gave him no clout at all with the planning people, but, in fact, the reverse was the case:

> They had to be seen as whiter than white and couldn't be seen as exercising favouritism. Eventually we struggled through and my application was finally granted after some

extremely contentious issues. The neighbours' objections didn't stand in the end, but I had to modify my plans and send a copy of the design to all the neighbours. One wanted to keep the views she already had, even though nobody has any right to a view unless they own the land, but, since then, half of them have died and the others have moved on.

The importance of assembling a good team

I had a very clear idea of what I wanted and we got started. I dug the foundations myself and got builders in to help me. We all worked like stink. The main builder is a friend and I believe it's difficult to undertake this kind of project otherwise. All the good builders round here own a lot of property themselves and they rip people off as they want to make a lot of profit. It's essential to get a builder you can trust and also essential to know exactly what you are doing and how much things actually cost.

The other important thing is to get a plumber and electrician lined up at a very early stage: 'For this project, the plumber cost £8,000 and the electrician, £11,000. You have to think on your feet as, if you get it wrong, you may not be able to put it right – especially when it comes to plumbing and wiring. They do say that your third self-build home will be your right home. The thing to keep in mind is that any deviation from a square box costs money.'

Making self-build pay

The house cost £180,000 to build and Mike reckons that it is now worth £500,000:

The right location is essential. You have to build where people want to be. Also, you must live in a self-build yourself to make it pay. If you buy to sell, you mustn't put in your personal taste and that is very difficult. We did this house as neutrally as we could and the décor is extremely bland. From a design point of view, you have to know what works and you learn this with experience.

Are they happy with the finished result?

When I met Mike and Tricia, they had been in the house just eight weeks and it was absolutely immaculate everywhere. There was no builder's rubble, the garden had been landscaped and, as a bonus, a pheasant sauntered across the lawn as if he owned the place. The house took just under a year to build, but it took six months for the gas pipes to be laid: 'The gas was a nightmare,' Mike shudders, 'there is just one company doing it and they make all the rules.'

Most of Devon is uPVC window country, even the character properties, and Mike's house also has uPVC windows: 'My brother was distraught when I said I was having plastic, as he has a conservatory company and hates plastic, but I wanted low maintenance. The overhang is wood and that is my only indulgence, but that will need maintenance.'

The worst thing, he said, was having to add disabled access: 'We had to have a ramp and, of course, this was more money. We also had to have at least one bath – we could not have all en suite shower rooms.'

One thing Mike has not compromised on is storage, which is often a problem in British homes. There are huge mirrored wardrobes everywhere and a utility room downstairs. Several people have commented that the house looks like a US home and it has certainly taken on board all the sensible US ideas, such as roomy garage space, en suites for every bedroom, lots of storage and space generally so nothing feels cramped.

When is a self-build not a self-build?

For many people, self-build is not literally a matter of digging your own foundations, laying each brick yourself and putting on the roof slate by slate with your own bare hands. What it means, in effect, is that you buy a plot of land and then get an architect or builder to design a house to your own specifications, which you then employ a team of builders to construct. There may be some DIY involved, depending on how skilled you are, but, in most cases, self-build consists of supervising your own individual house stage by stage.

If you prefer, you can buy a kit and build your own house, rather like assembling a doll's house. Most self-builders worthy of the name, however, do not consider buying prefabricated kits to be the real thing at all. As with other kits, you can get 'starter kits' for the first-time self-builder, progressing to complicated kits for the more advanced practitioner.

Planning permission

Building your own house is a major project, with many issues to consider. In most cases, you cannot just buy a plot somewhere and build what you like. Most self-builds turn out to be very problematic and experts advise not embarking on the enterprise in the first place unless you anticipate problems and are confident of your ability to deal with them.

Everything needs permission, so it's worth thinking about it in advance. For instance, is the self-build going to mean a change of use, as when a barn is converted into living accommodation, or a new address? Unless your self-build home is going to be in the middle of acres of land, you will probably also need to obtain permission from neighbours to put up scaffolding, have skips or cages on site or you may have to go across other people's land to access your own property.

The utilities

If the plot is miles away from anywhere, you may have to install a septic tank or get mains water laid on. Other utilities, such as gas and electricity – things we tend to take for granted – may also involve having to have pipes or wires laid at vast expense. In some outlying areas, it may not be possible to connect to the gas mains at all for the central heating and hot water. In this case, you may have to have gas provided in the form of expensive huge bottles that have to be regularly replaced or else opt for an oil tank.

The plots

Available plots of land are very often situated in places where nobody wants to live. One reason for this is that professional developers are always looking for spots where they can build a small estate or row of townhouses and they may snap up these plots several years before they actually want to build. Apart from disappearing quickly, such plots are not cheap either because of the demand. So, if you want a single plot, you may get the ones nobody else is interested in – far away from main transport links, schools, shops and other facilities.

Use the internet, lodge your interest with estate agents, keep your eyes and ears open and think creatively and eventually you will be lucky if you're persistent.

Such is the demand for development plots for self-build projects that they are becoming extremely expensive and also difficult to find. It is not unusual for buyers to have to spend £500,000 or more just for half an acre of land.

James Greenwood, of Stacks Property Search and Acquisition, who often buys plots for clients, offers the following advice:

First of all, speak to estate agents in the area you are searching. They may have plots for sale, or can give you leads. Talk to the planning department of the council, as they may know of sites where planning permission has been applied for, or granted.

Drive slowly round the area you are interested in, looking for 'infill' plots, particularly those at the edge of built-up areas, and also knock on doors and ask questions.

Keep looking in local papers for planning information and auction ads. Very many plots of building land are sold at auction. Above all, don't underestimate the overall cost of the project.'

For example, James Greenwood bought an acre of land in Bristol for a client for £600,000. 'You need patience and tenacity when looking for the ideal development plot', he said.

Skills needed

Although you will most probably be employing a wide range of skilled professionals, you will also need to call on many of your own skills before embarking on such a huge project. First of all, you will need design and project-managing skills. Although you may employ designers and architects, they will be working to what you want and most self-builders have a potent dream of what they want – a dream that they may have been carrying around in their heads for years.

You also have to be able to organize difficult, costly and frustrating elements, such as an aspect of permission suddenly being refused, builders not turning up, costly delays happening all the time and regular visits from a building control inspector who may not be pleased with what he sees.

Possible problems

The bigger the project, the more there is to go wrong and the more difficult it becomes to keep your temper, especially if you are living in temporary accommodation during the build. As always, there are likely to be communication problems with the builders. One couple, whose self-build costs came to far more than they imagined or had budgeted for, got together with their builders to see why the work was so much more expensive than originally quoted. They were given six main reasons for the extra costs, of which the main one was that changes kept being requested without understanding of the financial implications of these changes.

To this, the self-builders countered that they could not be expected to be experts in every aspect of the project as they were doing this for the first time.

Another bone of contention was that the site was not easily accessible and so it was expensive to transport materials and men on to the site. The self-builders argued here that the site was as easily accessible during the work as before – in other words, the site had not mysteriously moved – so how did this constitute extra cost?

Another argument the builders put forward was that special equipment had to be hired that they had not envisaged being needed at the beginning of the work. Also, the contractors argued, the site had to be decontaminated to make it habitable and this also had huge extra financial implications. Then there were also far more lorryloads of soil to be removed than envisaged. Finally, the building control department had demanded extra work be done, which was very expensive – work that was not included in the original quote. The contractors also maintained that, because of the extra work, the total number of man hours vastly exceeded that specified in the original quote.

The couple involved said that they believed their builders had known about these extras or, at any rate, should have done, but they were also angry with themselves for not fully questioning every aspect of the quote before work started. They also felt aggrieved that the builders had not given them monthly invoices or kept them informed, but, instead, issued just one enormous invoice at the end of the work.

This kind of problem is extremely common, given the vast emotional and financial complexity of self-builds, but it is made even worse by the general disinclination of builders and their clients to communicate at every stage. With a self-build, it is even more important than usual to keep a daily list, visit the site all the time and ask questions continually. There is a lingering feeling on the part of many self-builders that the contractors should know their job, but the builders are likely to be coming up against unforeseen snags all the time and have to get on. Also, they are often not the best communicators in the world, so self-builders need to make the effort to find out what is happening and keep an eye on things.

A major difficulty that can occur with a self-build is that of falling out with the builders, as it may be difficult, if not impossible, to get new builders to come in and pick up where the previous ones left off. As a self-builder, if you get a reputation for being difficult, word soon travels along the grapevine and may mean no reputable firm will touch you – they can do without the hassle.

The sorts of unforeseen problems that can occur include the staircase having to be fireproofed, the method of construction you have decided on meaning that you are unable to get a mortgage, funds running out extremely quickly and it being difficult to access more and the rooms not turning out as you had envisaged. For instance, it is very common for self-builders to have a vision of how their house is going to look, only to find that the reality is that it comes out smaller than they had expected, even though the builders have worked to the exact measurements. It is not always easy to imagine what the finished result will look like when all you have to go on is a mass of drawings.

There may also be problems with materials disappearing from the site. Security may not be particularly tight if a site is currently uninhabited.

A self-build undoubtedly takes over your whole life while it is in progress and it is more common than not for the carefully planned budget to go through the (unfinished) roof. It is also the case, say self-builders, that you will undoubtedly have to make compromises along the way. You may not get the ceiling height you wanted or the size kitchen you dreamed of, say. Very few self-builds ever work out perfectly and there is no doubt that you have to be a particular kind of person for it to work for you.

Bungalow gobbling

The 1930s was the heyday of the bungalow. In many parts of the country, you can see row upon row of dismal one-storey homes that nobody in their right minds would want to live in today.

However, bungalows now have a new use – as land. Because of tough planning restrictions on new builds and the scarcity of land, more and more people are buying bungalows with the intention of knocking them down completely and building a brand new house in their place or even several new houses. Many bungalows, although they may be horrible in themselves, are on prime plots in wonderful positions.

If a bungalow was poorly built, as a lot were, being little better than a prefabricated unit that came in kit form, there may be little sense in trying to modernize it. It may be better to demolish it and start again.

Planning permission

In theory, it should be easier to obtain planning permission for a house where there was already one standing than to build on an empty plot. However, as ever, it is vital to check with the local council as to what sort of new homes might be allowed and what restrictions there are on construction, height, size and so on. Some councils do not allow any significant increase in floor area, so you may have to build up, which would make your new home stand out from the other bungalows in the row. For this reason, some councils will require you to replace the existing bungalow with a 'bungalow-like' building so that it fits in with its surroundings.

Where planning permission is required, as it always will be with projects like these, neighbours might well object. One Bungalow Bill, Tony Addinall, wanted to knock down a tatty but large bungalow on a half-acre plot in Surrey and in its place build two large, detached, two-storey houses. He received outline planning permission in advance of the purchase and assumed all was fine, but, before work began, a neighbour wrote a 70-page letter to the council to express concern about the proximity of the projected new houses to his own dwelling. The council took the neighbour's objections seriously and planning permission was refused.

Tony had not reckoned on this and had to appeal and re-appeal. By the time he eventually obtained permission, he had incurred significant expenses. Although he had originally planned to live in one of the new houses himself, he could no longer bear to contemplate living there following all the fuss.

Neighbours who have happily lived in their bungalows for many years often do not take kindly to an outsider wanting to knock a neighbouring bungalow down to build a much bigger, two-storey house in its place. They are even less likely to be enthusiastic about a mini-housing estate being squashed in next to them. It is prudent to discuss your plans with them and get them on side as much as possible in the planning stages.

Financing the build

When buying a bungalow or, indeed, any other property with the intention of knocking it down and starting it again, you have to make sure that all the right financial arrangements are in place. As with any self-build project, financing it may well mean that you have to have quite a lot of capital yourself. It can also be difficult to find a lender that will allow demolition. The Ecology Building Society, for instance, will not fund the replacement of already viable buildings.

Then there is the question of VAT. If you leave some of the existing house in place, the project will most probably count as a restoration rather than a self-build and so will attract 17.5 per cent VAT. If you completely demolish an existing building and start again, you will probably be VAT-exempt. This is, of course, why many people prefer the second option.

As all self-build projects are incredibly expensive, it is vital to do all the research into planning, finance and possible neighbour objections before shelling out huge sums on the bungalow. Tony Addinall, for instance, bought his tatty bungalow for £355,000 – hardly a knockdown price, even though he was going to knock it down.

To give an idea of the kind of sums involved with self-build projects, here are some figures from *Homebuilding and Renovation* magazine.

A three-storey, eight-bedroom beach house in Bexhill-on-Sea cost £500,000 to buy the original house and £800,000 to completely rebuild and redesign it. The total cost, therefore, was £1.3 million, but the finished house was valued at £1.5 million.

Coming down the scale somewhat, a young couple – Mat and Ruth Cole – paid £30,000 for a plot in Devon and the building costs came to £148,000, making a total of £178,000. The finished house was immediately valued at £375,000.

A barn conversion in the New Forest cost £212,000 for the land and £160,000 for the build, making a total of £372,000. The completed conversion was immediately valued at £875,000.

A former agricultural building cost £265,000, with the building costs coming to another £151,917, making a total of £416,917. The conversion, in the Bristol area, was revalued at £1.2 million when all the work had been completed.

Capital gains tax

The advantages of self-build over property development, as such, is that, if you are building the place with the intention of living there or as your own home, you do not qualify for capital gains tax. If you are self-building with property development in mind and the house is not your main place of residence, then you will have to pay this tax. Some people build their own houses, live in them for a bit and then sell them on, usually for a profit.

Relying on profit

Although self-build homes are often valued at twice the price of the build, it has to be remembered that the property market fluctuates so much that any valuation means very little until it has actually sold. Also, self-build projects do not automatically go for double the total price of the build. Maurice and Rose Sumner's build in Wiltshire cost £461,000 and the house was revalued at £500,000 – not much more than it cost to do and that was not including the considerable amount of time they spent on in. In this case, too, the architect's fee came to £26,000.

Barn conversions

Many people like the idea of doing up a barn and they do make wonderful-looking homes, but what is the reality of buying, converting and living in a former barn? After all, barns are buildings that were not originally intended for human habitation.

First steps

First of all, you will need an architect to draw up plans and discuss what is and is not possible. You will certainly need planning permission and may need to have water and other utilities piped in. Also, be aware that the locals might object to an old barn or other derelict building being turned into living accommodation for smart urbanites. Because of the possibility of such objections, it makes sense to go and see the planners before buying, to make sure that their wishes can be accommodated and you are happy with any modifications they insist on, at the outset.

It is also a good idea to do what the Franks did, which was to involve the neighbours right at the start. If you get your neighbours involved in the process, they are more likely to be on your side, which is a good place for them to start as they will find themselves living next to a noisy, dirty building site for months on end.

The pros and cons

The advantage of barns – at least old ones – is that they often yield huge living accommodation. They also often have beams, flagstones and other interesting features that make them unique properties. Equally, they can be difficult to adapt and, if you are not careful, look rather twee.

Mostly, an existing barn or other agricultural building, such as a former granary or oast house, will have to be gutted completely and the insides started again from scratch. There are always likely to be hidden problems with such difficult buildings and these are more easily addressed if tackled at the outset.

The walls of the building may well not have been constructed in a way that is suitable for living accommodation, so a further block wall may have to be built to create an insulation cavity. The roof will need to be properly insulated. If the property is situated by water, the walls may need to be tanked out in case of flooding. Where mains water cannot be laid on, you will need a septic tank and this can problematic.

One self-builder who converted a former granary said of the installation of its septic tank, 'As the property was close to the river, they had to dig two huge holes in the bank; one to put in concrete for the tank and the other to hold the water. I had to use a specialist company for this job and the work involved crossing the bridge over the river.' In this case, the septic tank alone cost £3,500.

Most people who convert this type of building into a home prefer to use old, reclaimed bricks and floorboards to give a traditional look. This can also work out extremely expensive, adding another £20,000 or so on to the cost. In most cases, the materials needed for such conversions will be expensive and difficult to find. Self-builders wanting this look tend to become, if they weren't before, obsessive visitors of reclamation yards where they pounce on second-hand windows, tiles and bricks. The problem is always will there be enough old materials available to complete the job?

Most people undertaking major self-build projects, however, combine the old with the new. They tend to like old beams, old floorboards and old bricks, but may use MDF in the kitchen, for instance. Self-build projects often result in huge kitchens, enormous bathrooms and bedrooms and vast living rooms, all of which are far bigger than you could ever normally get in any other kind of home. In fact, it is usually the size that wins people over to this kind of self-build in spite of the time such a project takes and the amount of money it is likely to cost.

This is what Mike and Tricia Jordan have achieved. Their new house, though not a barn, is awesomely huge, with vast bedrooms and bathrooms and loads of storage. Also, because it is brand new, it can look absolutely 100 per cent – something you never get with old buildings. Mike has put in an immense brick fireplace to give some character to the house and also has a wood-burning stove, which is something many people like. As an indulgence, he has installed sound systems in all the ceilings and lighting behind the wood-burning stove. These are touches that you could not achieve with a conversion or restoration as they would have to form part of the original design.

Another factor with self-build homes is that there may be more choice about the roof than otherwise. Property developer Ivan Twigden has gone in for an array of different roofs when building his new executive estate in Hertfordshire – some are slate, some pantiles. Mike Jordan also went to town on the roof, to give his self-build an individual touch.

Timber frame houses

When people talk about property as an investment, they often speak of putting their money into bricks and mortar. Few people talk about getting into timber frames. Yet, timber frame homes are becoming ever more popular with self-build enthusiasts and there are several good reasons for this.

The pros and cons

Those unused to building their own homes often feel happier working with timber than bricks as bricklaying is a highly skilled job. Then there's the fact that timber frame houses often come in kit form, which means that they are often as easy to assemble as if they were made from Lego. Timber is light and easier to work with than bricks and mortar and insulation is easier, too. A big advantage is that they can be erected far more quickly than brick-built houses and do not need time to dry out as they are already dry. They are often cheaper than brick houses, too, and can incorporate a large number of individual requirements.

Computer-aided design has come to the aid of the timber frame home, so that now you can download your design and also customize it. Timber frame houses can also mimic many other types of houses, such as Tudor, brick-built, modern or traditional. They can be sprawling bungalows or several storeys high, look like barns or resemble a neat semi, country cottage or modern and minimal.

Yet, for all this, much prejudice lingers (in the UK, at least) concerning timber frame houses. There is a perception that timber is a cheap substitute for brick and the 'log cabin' connotations linger. There is also a belief that timber frame homes do not last as long as 'proper' brick-and-mortar ones. Timber frame houses are sometimes associated with a definite lack of aesthetics – with a greenhouse look.

In the UK, the brick-and-block type of house construction has always been preferred to the timber frame option. For some reason, timber frame construction has always had a downmarket image in the UK, but it is one that the timber frame industry is currently working hard to overturn.

The entire industry was given a nasty setback in 1983 when a *World in Action* programme stated that timber frame houses were far more liable than brick ones to have incurable damp problems.

Although a later report showed that this was not the case, the damage had been done.

Maybe the prejudice is simply because, in the UK, the population is resistant to wooden houses, anyway, which are popularly seen as being akin to cattle sheds. The truth is, timber frame houses have become so clever that, in the main, the ordinary observer would probably never know that they were timber frame. An advantage is that they tend to be easier to maintain and repair than brick-built houses. Indeed, Professor John Bellamy – an English academic who moved to Canada in the early 1970s – says that, 'Repairing and improving your property is not too difficult in North America as houses are timber frame, not brick, and any brick is one layer thick and cosmetic only.'

There are now many timber frame companies in the UK that will supply the basics needed for your self-build and advise on every aspect of building your very own wooden dream home, including choosing a plot and obtaining finance.

In Scotland, 96 per cent of self-builders now use timber frames. In England and Wales, acceptance has been slower, but the latest estimates say that 23 per cent of self-builders are now using timber frame construction.

On average, timber frame homes are completed two months quicker than brick homes and this, according to timber frame manufacturers, is a great plus, as a quicker self-build time keeps mortgage lenders happy.

They also say that timber frame houses are more energy efficient and do not emit CO_2 gas into the atmosphere. Although trees are cut down to make the frames, they come from renewable softwood sources, which absorb more carbon dioxide than younger trees, so they are ecologically sound.

Maybe those for whom timber frame is akin to tasteless cladding and uPVC windows will never be persuaded, but the concept is making self-build a reality for many people who would never otherwise have dared to contemplate building their very own home.

Self-build for profit?

Some people have been so badly bitten by the self-build bug that no sooner have they finished one customized home, than they are eager to start another. By contrast, others have been so traumatized by the whole thing that they never want to have anything to do with self-build ever again. Either way, does self-build mean that you can make a profit and is it a good way of property developing? Most people self-build homes to live in or for their own use, so they are unlikely to be subject to capital gains tax when they sell, unlike the average developer.

Although most self-builders are not in the game for instant profit, such homes, according to *Build It* magazine, tend to be worth around 30 per cent more when finished than they cost to build. It is difficult to ascertain whether or not they represent value for money until they are finished and the self-builder knows how it compares in price with similar homes in the area.

Because the self-built house tends to be unique – and larger and better appointed than those built by commercial developers – it will tend to attract a premium. The fact that these homes have usually been lovingly built by the owner also gives them a cachet that the ordinary developer's house, thrown up in an instant, would not possess.

Perhaps the best advice to self-builders is not to do it for immediate profit, as you will be up against all the developers that build new housing estates and can churn them out much cheaper. However, the bonus is that, should you want to sell, you will almost certainly not lose money and may well make some, enabling you to tackle your next self-build.

8 Finishing touches

It is the finishing touches, the attention to detail and quality that will set your renovation, extension or development apart from the rest. So many people seem to give up and run out of energy (and money!) just before the end and leave the project three-quarters finished. All estate agents and house makeover experts agree that this is the worst thing you can do, as it immediately gives a 'can't be bothered' look to the end result. If you can't be bothered to finish it, why should they be bothered to buy it?

If you are developing for profit, it is important to pay at least some attention to the garden or space in front of the building so that people aren't put off before they start. In an apartment block, too, the first thing people see is the entrance, so make sure that it looks smart and not as if you are spoiling the ship for a ha'porth of tar.

Attention to the end result means thinking about the whole project from beginning to end before you start, even if you cannot afford to have the whole thing done in the one hit. Thinking the whole thing through enables you to aim at a streamlined look throughout – and it is the followed through look, rather than bittyness, that impresses these days.

Having said that, it is important to cost in the finishing touches at the outset as, if you are not careful, they can be very expensive. Not long ago, I was looking round the show home of an exclusive new development in Hertfordshire. The five-bedroomed homes in a carefully landscaped setting were on the market for an average of £600,000 – a lot of money. The developer told me that the show home had cost around £60,000 to stage and it couldn't have been done for any less if they were to attract the right kind of buyer.

When renovating or developing, the trick is to make a list of all the finishing touches that you will need and put them into your initial project budget. Then, source them and allow enough money before you start – such things as doorknobs, curtains, proper locks and security measures, for instance. There may be ways in which you can cut corners as the project develops, but, if you leave absolutely no money for finishing off, then it will never look its best.

Doors

In the main, try to retain original doors unless these are absolutely horrible. Even 1930s-style doors now look quaint and entirely appropriate in 1930s properties. Avoid the temptation to put in uPVC front doors, especially in a character building, as they look truly terrible. A good front door is an enormous asset and will, of course, give the property that essential 'kerb appeal' when you come to sell.

Professor Brading's story

In November 2005, Alison Brading, an Oxford professor, was ordered to pay a £330 fine and £1,797 costs by magistrates for breaching conservation laws by replacing a wooden door with a plastic equivalent in her Grade II listed Oxfordshire cottage.

Professor Brading, who suffers from polio and has to use a wheelchair, argued that the plastic door was easier for her to open than the previous heavy wooden door and that in any case she had tried hard to find a plastic door that would not look too different from the original wooden one.

Cherwell District Council first raised the matter with Professor Brading when she failed to obtain retrospective planning permission for the new door in 2001. She appealed, but her appeal was dismissed on the grounds that the new door was an 'alien feature'. In September 2003 Professor Brading was fined £50 and ordered to pay £50 costs and also change the door, which she refused to do, saying that a new wooden door of the type stipulated would cost £3,000.

The point of this story is that, even with your own home, you cannot replace doors and windows with plastic if your home is listed or in a conservation area – at least not without listed building permission. Professor Brading's argument that she was disabled and wanted to carry on living in the house as long as possible did not move the magistrates.

But – is a plastic door really easier than a wooden door to open? Not really, as all plastic doors have to have steel reinforcements inside. Plastic doors are not appreciably lighter than wooden doors; their only advantage is that they are often more secure, as a steel panel goes down the side of the door that locks. A more recent addition to home improvement disasters than uPVC windows, plastic doors are gradually gaining acceptability.

Even so, they are bound to devalue a property, and many discerning buyers will not even enter a property that has a plastic door.

First impressions do count

A well-presented front door suggests a well-maintained house and, as we all know, first impressions count for more than anything else when buying property. Estate agents say that, very often, people will drive past the house before they decide whether or not to view it and, if the front door is dirty and unattractive, they will be put off and probably not even bother to go and have a look at the inside. I see so many expensive conversions and developments where no trouble at all has been taken with the appearance of the front door and it's a shame as this seemingly insignificant detail is actually very important.

How do you choose the right door?

The secret of getting the right door is to go with the period and character of the house. As a general rule, if the original door is still there, always repair rather than replace it – even if it is in poor condition. This is the case with more modern properties as well as Georgian and Victorian homes, as the original front door is part of the general look of the house. If it has long gone, try to recreate it or find a new door as near as possible to the original. For inspiration, look along your street at other houses similar to yours. In some cases, it may well be worth having a new door made to match the look of the original.

One builder told me to beware of apparently cheap front doors from out-of-town DIY stores as, by the time the door has been transported, cut to fit, had locks and door furniture fitted and been painted and sanded, the cost is often close to that of having a door custom-made as all these details will be included in the price. The piece of wood, he said, is only the start of what eventually becomes a front door.

Fanlights and leaded or stained glass are also part of the look of the door and, again, should be repaired rather than replaced. They should never be painted over, as this looks terrible and unwelcoming. Equally, never put glass panels in a door not originally designed to have them as they will always look wrong.

If your property is listed, you will not be able to put in just any old front door. In this case, you must consult your local council's conservation officer to see what kind of door is permitted.

To paint or not to paint

If a door was originally meant to be painted, then keep it painted and resist the temptation to strip and varnish it. The only doors that should be left bare and varnished, apart from some more modern examples, are Arts and Crafts-type doors and these are not common. Usually, stripped front doors do not look right.

Also, pay careful attention to the colour of the door. In the main, go for muted colours rather than garish hues. The right door furniture is also important. Cast iron often works better than brass, which tarnishes, unless you're prepared to keep them shiny. Make sure the locks are adequate and, if you need to replace them, remove all traces of the old locks and any other fittings for a clean look – vestiges of old fittings make a door look worn and unattractive.

Door furniture

Pay close attention to the letter box. It should be positioned in the middle of the door – not right at the top or bottom – and of a modern size. Many old-fashioned letter boxes are very small and do not accommodate today's mail. Get the biggest letter box you can find, so long as it is in proportion with the rest of the door.

Internal doors

Make sure that the internal doors are as near to the original type as possible, too. Most commonly in Victorian houses, but in houses of the 1930s and other eras as well, often you will find that they have had hardboard put on them – take it off. In the 1950s, magazines advised their readers to cover old-fashioned doors with hardboard to give a smooth-lined, modern touch. They now look horrible and, if you strip the stuff away from Victorian doors, you will probably discover that the panelling underneath is intact.

Door furniture on Victorian doors should be white, simple and ceramic or traditional brass. Finger plates give a luxury touch and are much appreciated. Patterned knobs and finger plates now look dated. Paint the doors in eggshell gloss and, if you want to follow the professionals' advice, use oil-based eggshell rather than water-based, even though it is more difficult to apply than water-based paint.

In conversions and apartment blocks, you may be forced to fit fire doors. Unfortunately, in the main, these are horrible. It may be worth buying fake mouldings, if you have to fit fire doors, but, if so, check very carefully that they are straight. Wonky fake moulding looks truly dreadful, but, in some old buildings nothing is straight, so you have to make a decision as to which lines to go with.

Cheap interior doors look cheap, but, where cost is a factor, always go for the plainest ones that you can find. Any curlicues or patterns immediately cheapen them. It is worth visiting salvage yards to look for old doors when you are working on a period property.

It is also important to pay attention to the way in which the doors are hung and whether they open into the room or out of it. Doors that open into bathrooms or small rooms can make them seem much smaller and limit your options for placing furniture and fittings. Equally, if a lot of doors open outwards, they could keep banging together. One solution where space is tight is to have sliding doors or maybe even concertina doors. At any rate, try not to take away valuable space by having doors opening in awkward directions.

Windows

Nowadays, we all seem to want to have more light and, to achieve this goal, the bigger the windows the better. However, there are restrictions on the window size and type allowed in some properties, especially listed buildings and those in conservation areas. New buildings often have restrictions on window size imposed on them for a different reason – so as to conserve energy. This is why you so often see little windows in new houses.

So, as with other elements of your project, before going to the trouble and expense of fitting new windows, make sure that the design and style you have in mind is permitted.

A reputable builder will often undertake the job of putting in new windows, but you may decide to use a specialist company instead. The Glass and Glazing Federation insists on a strict code of practice for its members, who can advise you on the right type of glass for your project and ensure that it meets current regulations.

Are uPVC windows ever OK?

A survey, referred to earlier, found that replacement uPVC windows in period buildings significantly reduced their value in the eyes of buyers. The secret is to ensure that all windows, glass doors and other glass elements are in keeping with the character of the building. Personally, as you will no doubt have picked up on by now, I do not like uPVC windows, but the reality is that they are extremely common in modern buildings. Even new buildings that mimic a Regency or Georgian style will most likely have uPVC windows. The only time modern buildings have wooden windows is when developers prefer them or local planning departments insist on them.

All renovation and makeover experts, however, would agree with the above survey and maintain that uPVC windows in a period or character property take away much of its value.

Extensions and conservatories look far better when constructed of wood than when made from uPVC – and also add more value to the property. The uPVC conservatory is another value-decreasing item.

It is often said that, had uPVC been available for windows in Victorian times, then Victorian builders would have used them. However, the fact is, they didn't and uPVC windows in old properties hardly ever look good. The trouble with them is that they are so very visible – other modern touches are more out of sight, but windows are one of the first things you notice about a property.

The other thing about uPVC is that it does not last forever – it will degrade after 20 or 30 years and look dingy and terrible. The idea that uPVC is maintenance-free is a myth. Well, that is, you may not need to paint it, but it is by no means everlasting. By contrast, wooden sash windows are often operating as good as new a century after they were installed.

Some practical considerations

Architects and designers can fall out with clients over windows, as architects are often so fixated on style and appearance that they forget windows need to be opened and curtained. Never go for windows that make it difficult to hang curtains or blinds, as in some 1960s and 1970s buildings, where windows open on a swivel, half in and half out of the room. They are a nightmare. If you are having new windows fitted, make sure that they just open outwards, not both inwards and outwards. The type that open inwards take away some of the size of the room. Sash windows are hard to beat, but they are not suitable for all types of property. All French doors should open outwards.

If you are planning a major conversion, or even just having new windows, make sure that the design you choose can comfortably accommodate curtains and/or blinds. You can get special blinds for Velux windows that are attached to the actual frame or glass, but, for ordinary windows, think about window covering at the same time as the actual windows.

Double glazing

A member of the GGF will be able to tell you whether or not your windows need to be double-glazed as there are now strict regulations about this, even for period properties. Whatever you do, never be swayed by double-glazing salespeople or cold callers. These people are all on commission and will try any tactic to gain a sale and the products may be of dubious quality. It's up to you if and when you replace windows, not them, so take no notice of the 'discounts' they offer. Anyway, many of the DIY superstores offer windows at far lower prices than companies offering supposed discounts.

Getting quotes and warranties

When replacing windows, get up to 10 quotes as prices vary wildly. One person had quotes of between £7,000 and £18,000 for the same windows. New wooden windows cost more than uPVC but are the only way to go in a character property.

It is useful to know that you should never buy guarantees or warranties offered with new windows as they will be insured under your general household policy, so it is a waste of money taking out separate insurance for them.

Security

When renovating in city areas, people often go for security grilles. The street I live in has security grilles up at most windows. To my mind, they look absolutely dreadful – as if you live in a prison. Double glazing with efficient window locks is more effective security and looks so much better.

Blinds and curtains

Fashions in blinds and curtains are changing all the time and what looked good a decade ago, however expensive and upmarket it was at the time, may now look very dated.

Introducing the New Unique Range
of Solid Oak Flooring from Millennium Hardwoods

We go to great lengths to ensure high quality of the timber – we source our own from sustainable forests and always from the same country providing consistency of colour. We have a fully automated, purpose built flooring production line. Our flooring is planed to EXACT parallel and thickness dimensions thus giving a flatter board enabling straighter tongues and grooves. The result is faster, easier fitting and less cost. Machining to order ensures our flooring is a better fit and is more attractive.

The flooring is sanded prior to finishing. End matching; the end of board tongues and grooves, is mechanically totally variable and not geared to specific lengths providing faster production speeds and much greater accuracy. Each each board is individually inspected and another automated process sprays lacquer on to ALL edges of the board sealing it to keep moisture out. We also offer a selection of different lacquers and finishes.

So, apart from the fact that we can now offer a far superior high end product at much the same price as other hardwood flooring suppliers, what makes our flooring so much better?

- The lacquer we use is oil based – it penetrates into the wood. It won't chip and if dented it can simply be sanded or planed to restore it back to pristine condition.
- If the flooring is severely scratched, our 2 part polish will repair it. Conventional U.V. lacquer is almost impossible to repair.
- Because we use a unique oil based lacquering process we do not have to cut "v" grooves in our flooring, so no dust traps.
- Our boards are bigger ranging from 1500mm to 3000mm in length and from 115mm to 200mm in width resulting in a much more traditional English look, plus easier and quicker installation.
- If your flooring suffers a major trauma you can come back to us, the manufacturers, and replace the damaged board with exactly the same product, guaranteed to match the flooring you originally bought.

Finally, if you need any advice at all, simply pick up a telephone and speak to us. We're more than happy to advise and recommend a solution to your particular problem or circumstance. We guarantee you will not be speaking to an automated call centre but a member of our team with an in-depth knowledge of the product.

When planning any renovation, think about the kind of window covering that would best suit the property. There is often a temptation to go for the cheapest solution, as, by the time you come to curtains, you may be running very short of money. Developers often skimp on curtains and this is frequently a giveaway sign that a developer has renovated a house. To take away that 'developer look', make sure that the curtains are of a good quality and full length. Sill-length curtains, in most situations, look mean and cheapen the property.

If you can afford it, have made-to-measure curtains rather than buying ready made, which never quite fit and look cheap and skimpy. The best curtains are interlined as well as lined; this gives them a heavy, substantial look. Another benefit is that good-quality curtains conserve warmth and last for years – longer, probably, than a kitchen or bathroom.

I may be biased, but I think good curtains absolutely make a room and give such a wonderful first impression that you can skimp on furniture. Whenever I look at upmarket show homes, the curtains are always a delight. Good curtains can give a luxurious look to even the most ordinary property.

Flooring

The choice of flooring is huge and has never been greater. The choice of prices is huge, as well. Although the look is undoubtedly important, as flooring is extremely visible, it is also vital to go for a type of flooring that will stand up to hard wear as, inevitably, all floors get a thorough bashing over the years.

Stone can make a home look cold. It is expensive and always cold underfoot. Wooden floors can look extremely stylish, but are best kept for downstairs.

Before buying any type of flooring, check what maintenance is required. The fact is, nobody wants to be on their hands and knees scrubbing floors all day long and so a high-maintenance floor will rarely get the kind of care it needs.

Carpet

Carpet has not been wildly fashionable in recent years, but it absorbs dirt, is soft underfoot and should last for many years. Carpet is also far quieter than wood or stone and more comfortable underfoot. Carpet is recommended for stairs and bedrooms. Don't be tempted to have wooden or laminate floors in upstairs rooms unless you are preparing the home for somebody with allergies as you will be able to hear every sound in the rooms below. Seagrass-type carpeting looks wonderful when new, but it cannot be cleaned and is not hardwearing.

Other options

Laminate floors are suitable for low-priced properties only and should never be laid in upmarket homes. Bathrooms should never have carpet – it just doesn't work. Lino, vinyl or stone, however, are perfect.

Fitting

Remember, whatever type of flooring you choose, it needs to be laid well. Choose fitters who belong to the National Institute of Carpet and Floor Layers as they have to pass written exams before being accepted as members (telephone: 0115 958 3077 or visit the website at: www.nicfltd.org.uk).

Fireplaces

All living rooms need a focal point and there is no doubt that attractive fireplaces give a property instant appeal. There is a huge choice of fireplaces and fire surrounds, plus gas and electric fires. Some are stylish and some are naff. As fireplaces are so visible, avoid the naff at all costs.

Original fireplaces – so long as they are not 1950s tiled jobs – will enhance a property. If the original fireplaces have all been removed, put ones back in if you can – especially in an older building. Obviously, the style of the fireplace should be in keeping with the style of the building and/or renovation.

Where they have survived, Victorian fireplaces should be allowed to remain. Gas fires look good, send out lots of heat and are easier to cope with than a real fire. Save real fires for the country as, although people like them in theory, the reality is that it's usually too much trouble to get them going on a regular basis.

Good mantelpieces and surrounds also enhance the look of a fireplace. Victorian properties with high ceilings and no fireplaces can look forbidding; fireplaces make a room look welcoming and cosy.

Lighting and other electrical considerations

Lighting

Lighting is so important that it should form an integral part of the general refurbishment work, rather than be an afterthought. If you are embarking on major work, think about the lighting before anything else and ask a qualified electrician about what is and is not possible. Very old properties will need rewiring anyway and this will need to be done at a very early stage – it cannot be done later – so it's best to think carefully about what you want right from the beginning.

The thing to make sure of is that you have enough light and enough variety of lighting. Many people do away with central lights, but, in homes with high ceilings, they can be an integral part of the décor. All central lights should be on a dimmer switch, then they can be low for general background lighting or bright when you need good light.

Consider useful details, too, such as whether or not you will need lights in fitted wardrobes and cupboards, outside or security lighting, what kind of lighting will create the best effect in bathrooms, given that there are stringent restrictions here, and so on.

Sockets and more sockets

You simply cannot have too many power points. In these high-tech times, we have so many things that need to be plugged in that thinking through carefully what you are going to use where will make all the difference to how easy or awkward the finished rooms will be to live in.

You will need to consider in which rooms internet access will be required. Wiring for satellite and cable TV is also a must in a modern home, but note that not all planning departments allow dishes on the outsides of buildings.

Painting and decorating

As this is usually done last of all and can eat up quite a large chunk of the budget, the temptation is to do it yourself, on the grounds that 'anybody' can paint and decorate. In fact, done properly, it is a very skilled job and well worth what it costs. Nobody has endless amounts of money, but there is also no doubt that a professional paint job makes a great deal of difference to the final look of the thing.

Note that most builders do not include painting and decorating in their quotes and many say that they don't get into this aspect of the work.

Very often when I view new developments or conversions, it is obvious that the painting has been done in a hurry and has never been quite finished. It is true that most householders can wield a paintbrush and, at a pinch, can do their own painting once the rest of the job has been completed. I must admit that I usually do my own painting as I have almost always run out of money by the time I've reached this stage. My paint job looks OK, but it is not done to the highest standards, simply because I don't have the expertise. The thing is that, when you paint rooms only once every decade or so, you do not build up the necessary skills, whereas the professionals have been trained and are doing it all the time, so become proficient at it.

I would say that it is worth getting the professionals in if you can afford it, but, if not, if you are reasonably good at it, this is one of the few jobs you can do yourself to save money without totally ruining the result.

If you don't know of any good painters and decorators in your area, a good place to start is to find a member of the Painting and

Decorating Association (telephone: 024 7635 3776 or visit the website at: www.paintingdecoratingassociation.co.uk).

Wallpaper and other decorative features

Whether or not you decide to have wallpaper depends on personal taste, the price level of the development or refurbishment and the market you are hoping to attract. I would say that, for upmarket properties, at least some wallpaper is essential, as it gives an opulent, luxurious feel to the home. Wallpaper looks good in halls and, indeed, in all rooms where you do not spend much time. Consider having some expensive wallpaper in a separate dining room, for instance. It lasts for years and looks comforting and welcoming.

Wallpaper really does need to be put on straight and in such a way that you can't see the joins. As with painting, it is a skilled job and should never be done by an amateur.

A bane of restorers' lives is old woodchip paper. It is best to strip this off if you can as, again, it looks terrible. It was generally used because the original plaster was in poor condition, so the denuded walls will most likely have to be papered again if they are not straight and smooth. In such cases, I would go for upmarket Anaglypta or similar.

If the property has been wallpapered all over in cheap, nasty or old-ladyish shiny paper, remove it or, if this is too expensive or difficult, paint over it with quick-drying eggshell – the only paint that covers shiny paper, eventually. In one of my flats, I had to put five coats of paint on before the wallpaper pattern disappeared, but, as the walls were very old and flaky elsewhere, I did not dare risk removing the wallpaper.

Ceiling treatments

Ceilings should always be plain, in any type of property, never Artexed. Experts say that Artex ceilings definitely cheapen a property. I cringe whenever I see the words 'textured ceilings' in estate agents' descriptions of properties as I know that this means hideous. Although it can be difficult to remove, ceilings can often be skimmed over instead to give a smooth look.

The other totally hideous ceiling treatment is polystyrene ceiling tiles – popular about 30 years ago, when they were used to hide a multitude of sins. As with Artex, they can be extremely difficult to remove. Take advice before removing them yourself, but do remove or hide them if at all possible.

There are now many companies offering Artex removal, and you can also get an Artex remover gel that – according to the manufacturers – allows texture to be scraped off easily from ceilings and walls using a paint scraper.

My own view is that removal of texture on ceilings or walls is a professional job and that, really, you need to call in the experts. Sometimes Artex or polystyrene is hiding a multitude of sins, and the walls and ceilings may need to be completely replastered once the texture has been removed.

Texture on walls or ceilings is no longer a good look – if ever it was – and should always form part of a renovation programme.

Cornicing

Cornicing is an important feature of older houses and looks good in more modern properties, too. If it has been removed, where possible, replace it as this gives a substantial and upmarket look to any property. You can get polystyrene cornicing, which looks OK when up, or proper plaster cornicing, which is preferable but more expensive. Also, it really does need to be put up by an expert as it is quite a fiddly and difficult job, but what a difference it makes!

If it overstretches the budget or for any other reason cornicing is not a viable option, paint the walls and ceiling in the same colour, so that you do not get the inevitably wobbly demarcation line. Very pale creams and neutrals can look good on ceilings as well as walls, but never opt for a dark or powerful colour if you are painting the ceiling in the same colour as the rest of the room.

Shelving and storage

Few people ever seem to give proper thought to shelving and storage and many developer's homes do not have enough of either. In fact, few developer's properties ever have any storage at all, apart from kitchen units. They are so keen to create space everywhere that they forget all about storage solutions, yet good shelving and storage absolutely sell a place and show that you have thought about where everything is going to go.

In general, fixed shelves and fitted wardrobes are preferable to freestanding versions and add rather than take away value. However, you have to be careful not to narrow your market by putting in too much shelving.

I would always put in fitted wardrobes where possible. If there is not room for a fitted wardrobe in a bedroom, it begs the question where is a freestanding one to go? There is nothing worse than a shop-type rail in one corner for clothes, especially if you are trying to sell the property. Unless yours is an especially high-spec renovation, you do not have to use expensive wood. Painted shelves and cupboards can look good, especially where they are painted the same shade as the walls, but make sure that shelves are chunky, not thin and mean-looking.

A good carpenter can make ready-made shelving fit and, for many projects, this can be the answer. Compare prices, though, to check that you will not end up paying more than if the shelving were to be custom-made.

Dressing and staging

Television makeover shows pay great attention to dressing and staging. This is partly because these final touches provide the wow factor that such shows always demand, but if you are developing for profit or getting a buy-to-let property up and running, what kind of staging is required?

In one recently developed house near me, the agents advised the developers to 'dress' the house, as it was not selling. Not really understanding what was required, they put vases of artificial flowers everywhere. As a neighbour said, it ended up looking like something out of the film *My Big Fat Greek Wedding* – and it still didn't sell!

The usual advice here is to give people an idea of the kind of lifestyle that they could have if they lived in the house. If an upstairs room can take a double bed, put one in to show that there's room for it. Downstairs, put in a dining table and chairs as, when viewing properties, the first question many people ask is 'Where would we eat?'

A sofa and coffee table make a room look welcoming and today's buyers expect curtains and flooring to go with the whole scheme as well. Beautiful rooms should not be empty as they actually look bigger when they are furnished or partly furnished. Big plants and fresh (not artificial!) flowers also look good, as do a few items in the kitchen.

If a room is intended as a study, put a desk and computer equipment or a filing cabinet in there. Tiny rooms too small for bedrooms or any other purpose often make ideal studies or they can do service as a gym. Putting an exercise bike and treadmill in a tiny box room also gives purchasers a sense of the property being up-to-date, in line with modern thinking.

One of my properties has a tiny room with only an internal window. It was probably a walk-in store cupboard, dating back to when the building was a hotel. When I bought the flat, this room was full of mess and clutter. I cleared it out and found that there was room for a small desk, chair, filing cabinet and shelving. Now it has become a study, which impresses visitors and would, I'm sure, impress buyers just as much. All developers say that most buyers have very little imagination and can't see for themselves how spaces could best be used. It is up to you, the developer or vendor, to show them.

Something else there should always be space for is a ladder, especially in high-ceilinged properties. If potential buyers can't see how they would manage to change a ceiling light bulb, they might decide that the property would be too difficult for them to manage and walk away without making an offer.

As for staging and dressing the property, one developer said, 'These days, everybody watches so many makeover shows that they are all too well aware of the tricks. Even so, they work!'

A property that is sensitively 'staged' always sells quicker than one left empty – and usually for more money. Don't forget that you can hire suitable furniture to stage a property – it could be money well spent, especially as you are not then left with furniture you don't want. Also, you should always dress a newly developed or converted property with new furniture, not hand-me-downs, so hiring can really help here.

Another aspect that sells is cleanliness. Make sure that all the windows are sparkling clean, doors are free of finger-marks and there is no visible builder's rubble lying around. If you can't face it yourself, it could be worth hiring a specialist firm to do it for you before putting the place on the market.

Putting in the finishing touches shows that you care, that you love property and are interested in giving value for money. These are the things that speak to buyers.

Just a few more points. If you are presenting a property to rent it out, always put in a potted plant or two and ensure that any rugs or mats are fresh and clean. In one of my rental properties, I have a large white rug from Ikea. This rug lasts about six months before it becomes dirty, when I throw it away and get another one. Although not practical, it absolutely makes the place and gives a clean, fresh impression when potential tenants are viewing.

Finishing touches are also important when you are renovating for your own use. Unfinished jobs make a place extremely depressing after a while and lower your enjoyment of your own home.

On my travels round the country viewing properties of all kinds, from dismal studios to grand mansions standing in their own grounds, I have seen everything from so clean and tidy that not even yesterday's newspaper is lying about to messy, untidy and bohemian. I think you can be too clean and tidy and need a little 'sweet disorder' to show that real human beings actually live there.

In general terms, the newer the property, the neater and cleaner it needs to be. Older properties can take an element of shabbiness as the reality is that it is impossible to have everything absolutely immaculate when it is old.

Conclusion

When I first started writing this book, you will recall, the scene outside my home resembled a particularly horrendous abandoned building site. Now that the book is finished, several months later, all the expensive renovations that my neighbours and myself were embarking on are also finished and we are happily living in our newly refurbished homes.

The value of the properties has probably shot up as a result of all this effort, but the greatest satisfaction lies in the vastly improved quality of life we are all enjoying in our homes as a result of our modernization and renovation programmes. Now that the last of the builders has left, the skips have been carted away, the scaffolding taken down and the rubbish and rubble have been removed – not to mention the sodden mattress, exploded television sets and broken kitchen units – we are all fast forgetting the trials and tribulations we endured along the way. Was it really only last year that the sole appliance in my kitchen was an ever-turning cement mixer and my only roof a flapping blue plastic tarpaulin?

Now that the work has been completed, it seems that the homes in my street have been improved as if by magic. That's how it is with successful work on your property – you live in dust and mess and dirt and mud for ages, think you can't stand it a minute longer and then, suddenly, the agony and trauma end, the builders disappear and you are left (with any luck) with a fabulous new bathroom, kitchen, extension, loft conversion or other delight.

Is the trend set to continue?

Because the results can be so gratifying, all the signs are that property renovation will continue to seduce and attract ever more people. The more you undertake, the more your confidence in being able to tackle the next, even bigger, job grows. Projects that once would have appeared impossibly daunting start to seem simple and ordinary, even everyday. However, every new project throws up its own challenges – not least of which are the arts of keeping your temper and your humour intact while your house is being demolished about your ears.

Even with all its complications and the expense, there is no doubt that property improvement is highly addictive. Maybe it's because there are few joys in life to compare with the heady pleasure of creating a truly beautiful home, whether it is for yourself or somebody else to live in. Most people who have accomplished one successful building project start to contemplate another once they have had a chance to recover from the ordeal.

One reason for property development in the UK being so very satisfying is that there are so many styles of architecture to choose from. You can go for a quaint medieval cottage in need of total renovation or undertake to restore a grand heritage building to its former glory. You can decide to improve and update a 1930s semi or buy a small bungalow and expand and modernize it. You can even choose to glamorize a basic 1960s council flat.

You can buy a non-residential building, such as a barn, oast house, former post office or fire station, to turn into an individual home. Alternatively, you can go the whole hog and buy a plot of land on which to build a unique dream dwelling.

You can renovate your own home for fun or you can become a property developer for fun plus (hopefully) profit.

Don't stop there!

Ever more people, fired up by home-grown renovation success, are now venturing abroad to do the same thing. In doing this, they are taking on the even more formidable challenges of tussling with foreign builders, coping with bewildering and illogical foreign planning departments and trying to find a path through unfathomable foreign rules and regulations. Some of those who have lived to tell the tale have written it down and their books make dramatic, heart-stopping reading.

Keep your feet on the ground

Having renovated many places myself over the years, I know how exciting and rewarding the job can be. I also know, from bitter experience, just how much careful planning is needed if you are to have a hope of getting the job done without having your nerves – and your bank balance – permanently shredded to pieces in the process.

I have also learnt the importance of banishing any fantasies or wishful thinking from my mind. Although successful renovation does involve a leap of the imagination, all the hard facts must be taken on board before ever embarking on an expensive project. It is no use just hoping that everything will turn out all right; you have to take account of as many certainties as you can beforehand and then mix these with a healthy dose of scepticism. All successful renovation projects have been subjected to constant reality checks.

It is vital to work out all the figures well in advance, including the sneaky ones such as estate agents' fees, capital gains tax, stamp duty, council tax and utility bills – all of which can be conveniently forgotten in the excitement of the moment. Then you have to make sure that you keep all the lines of communication open with everybody involved in the project. This means talking to the builders all the time, but also making sure that local planning departments and building inspectors are kept informed as well. Then, any neighbours have to be kept happy as they have the potential to turn round and completely scupper your plans. Make daily lists so that nothing slips through the net to become a problem that it is too late to rectify. Although you have to learn to think on your feet, as some decisions need to be made quickly, you also have to make time to weigh up all the options when you are not sure of the next step forward.

The recipe for success

The ingredients needed for successful property improvements are: first, the vision; second, the ability to plan everything in detail; third, enough money in place and, most of all, good advice from those who know, so I hope this book helps you on your way.

Directory

Good general books

Vorderman, Carol (1999) *Carol Vorderman's Better Homes*, Granada Media.

Beeny, Sarah (2003) *Profit from Property*, Cassell.

Cork, Alison (2000) *Alison Cork's Guide to Renovating Your Home*, Piatkus.

Llewelyn-Bowen, Laurence and Diarmuid, Gavin (2002) *Home Front Inside Out*, BBC.

Roper, Peter (1988) *A Practical Guide to Windows*, International Thomson Business Publishing.

Meany, Terry (2000) *The Complete Idiot's Guide to Plumbing*, Alpha.

Callo, Kat (2005) *Making Sense of Leasehold Property*, Lawpack.

Callo, Kat (2006) *The Survivor's Guide to Buying your Leasehold*, Lawpack.

Finding a location

Association of Relocation Agents
Tel: 0870 0737 475
Website: www.relocationagents.co.uk

National Association of Estate Agents
Tel: 01926 496800
Website: www.naea.co.uk

National Directory of Estate Agents
Tel: 01935 411165
Website: www.ukpropertyshop.com

National Housebuilding Council
Tel: 01494 735 363
Website: www.nhbc.co.uk

Assertahome
Tel: 020 7922 5064
Website: www.assertahome.com

Channel 4 Homes Property Search
Website: www.channel4.com/4homes

fish4
Tel: 020 8600 700
Website: www.fish4.co.uk

Homecheck
Website: www.homecheck.co.uk

Hometrack
Website: www.hometrack.co.uk

Property Price Advice
Website: www.propertypriceadvice.co.uk

Rightmove
Website: www.rightmove.co.uk

UK Villages
Tel: 01223 874500
Website: www.UKVillages.co.uk

UpMyStreet
Tel: 020 7802 2992
Website: www.upmystreet.com

Builders

National Federation of Builders
Tel: 020 7608 5150
Website: www.builders.org.uk

Federation of Master Builders
Tel: 0800 015 2522
Website: www.findabuilder.co.uk

Quality Mark scheme
Tel: 0845 300 8040 (hotline)
Website: www.qualitymark.org

UK Trades Confederation
Tel: 0870 9220 442
Website: www.uktc.org

Tasmen Construction
Tel: 020 8995 2162, mobile: 07775 656964
E-mail: info@tasmen.co.uk

Listed buildings

English Heritage
Tel: 0870 333 1181
Website: www.english-heritage.org.uk

Society for Protection of Ancient Buildings
Tel: 020 7377 1644
Website: www.spab.org.uk

Georgian Group
Tel: 020 7529 8920
Website: www.georgiangroup.org.uk

Victorian Society
Tel: 020 8994 1019
Website: www.victoriansociety.org.uk

Shows

The Homebuilder and Renovation Show
Tel: 020 7970 4249
Website: www.homebuildingshow.co.uk

The Property Investor Show
Tel: 020 8877 3636 (Homebuyer Events)
Website: www.propertyinvestor.co.uk

Magazine

Property Investor News
Tel: 020 8906 7772

Finance

Council of Mortgage Lenders
Tel: 020 7437 0075
Website: www.cml.org.uk

The Ecology Building Society
Tel: 0845 6745566
Website: www.ecology.co.uk

Lloyds TSB Scotland plc
Website: www.lloydstsb.com

Mortgage Guarantee PLC
Tel: 01744 886884
E-mail: loans@ecology.co.uk

Norwich and Peterborough Building Society
Tel: 0845 300 2522
Website: www.npbs.co.uk

Evening Standard
Website: www.thisismoney.com

Kitchens

Kitchen and Bathroom Specialists Association
Tel: 01905 726066
Website: www.kbsa.co.uk

The Bespoke Kitchen Company
Tel: 0800 169 3979
Website: www.thebkc.co.uk

Kitchen Clinic
Tel: 020 7924 7877
Website: www.kitchenclinic.co.uk

The Kitchen Studio
Tel: 0870 121 2115

Martin Moore
Tel: 0161 928 2643
Website: www.martinmoorekitchens.com

Smallbone of Devizes
Tel: 020 7589 5998
Website: www.smallbone.co.uk

Mark Wilkinson
Tel: 01380 850007
Website: www.mwf.com

Cookers

Aga-Rayburn
Tel: 0845 762 6147
Website: www.aga-rayburn.co.uk

Stoves
Tel: 0151 432 7849
Website: www.stoves.co.uk

Worktops

Granite Worktops Direct
Tel: 020 7012 1296
E-mail: sales@diapol.co.uk

The Granite Workshop
Tel: 01480 860088
Website: www.thegraniteworkshop.co.uk

Tuscan Marble
Tel: 01938 280324

Magazines

25 Beautiful Kitchens
E-mail: 25_beautiful_kitchens@ipcmedia.com

Kitchens, Bedrooms and Bathrooms
Tel: 020 8515 2000
E-mail: dmgworldmedia@subscription.co.uk

Move or Improve
Website: www.moveorimprove.co.uk

Bathrooms

Armitage Shanks
Tel: 01482 346461

Bathrooms@Source
Tel: 0800 870 0066
Website: www.bathroomsatsource.co.uk
E-mail: bathroomsatsource@hotmail.com

Heritage Bathrooms
Tel: 0117 963 3333
Website: www.heritagebathrooms.com

Ideal-Standard
Tel: 01462 346461
Website: www.ideal-standard.co.uk

Independent Bathroom Specialists Association
Tel: 0870 2408028
Website: www.ibsa.org.uk

Kaskade/Nor More Ply (STS)
Tel: 0800 0015 092

Twyford Bathrooms
Tel: 01270 87977
Website: www.twyfordbathrooms.com

Villeroy & Boch
Tel: 020 8871 4028
Website: www.villeroyboch.com
E-mail: bathinfo@villeroy-boch.co.uk

Water Front
Tel: 01865 371571
Website: www.waterfront.ltd.uk

Bath resurfacing

Brandon Marketing
Tel: 01302 788138
Website: www.brandonmarketing.co.uk

Storage solutions

The Holding Company
Tel: 020 8445 2888
Website: www.theholdingcompany.co.uk

Fireplaces

The National Fireplace Association
Tel: 0121 200 1310
Website: www.nationalfireplaceassociation.org.uk
E-mail: enquiries@nfa.org.uk

Antique fireplaces

The Edwardian Fireplace Company
Tel: 020 8995 2554
Website: www.edwardianfires.com

Nostalgia
Tel: 0161 477 7706

Flooring

Millennium Hardwoods
Tel: 0800 652 2475
Website: www.millenniumhardwoods.co.uk

National Institute of Carpet and Floor Layers
Tel: 0115 958 3077
Website: www.nicfltd.org.uk

The Alternative Flooring Company
Tel: 01264 335111
Website: www.alternativeflooring.com

The Natural Wood Floor Co.
Tel: 020 8871 9771
Website: www.naturalwoodfloor.co.uk

Carpets

The Carpet Foundation
Tel: 0845 601 2200
Website: www.comebacktocarpet.com

Floors Direct
Website: www.floorsdirect.co.uk

Loft conversions

Capital Loft Conversions
Tel: 0709 238 2252
E-mail: info@capitalloft.co.uk

Econoloft
Tel: 0800 269765
Website: www.econoloft.co.uk

Loft Centre Products
Tel: 01248 785 246
Website: www.loftcentreproducts.co.uk

The Loft Shop
Tel: 0870 604 0404
Website: www.loftshop.co.uk

Book

Williamson, Laurie (2000) *Loft Conversions: Planning, Managing and Completing Your Conversion*, Crowood.

Conservatories

Conservatory Land
Tel: 0800 952 8000
Website: www.conservatoryland.com

Portland Conservatories
Tel: 0800 269126
Website: www.portland-conservatories.co.uk

Garden design

Fake Landscapes (artificial garden specialists)
Website: www.fake.com

Martin Summers Gardens
Tel: 020 7978 5186

Self-build properties

Courses

Walter Segal Self Build Trust
Tel: 01905 749665
Website: www.segalselfbuild.co.uk

Magazines

Build It
Website: www.buildit-online.co.uk
E-mail: buildit@mrn.co.uk

Homebuilding and Renovating
Tel: 01527 834406
Website: www.homebuilding.co.uk

Packages

Custom Homes
Tel: 01787 377388
Website: www.customhomes.co.uk

Design and Materials
Tel: 01909 540 123
Website: www.designandmaterials.uk.com

Potton Ltd
Tel: 01480 401401
Website: www.potton.co.uk

Timber frame homes

UK Timber Frame Association
Tel: 0125 927 2140
Website: www.timber-frame.org

The National Homebuilding and Renovation Show
Tel: 0870 010 9031
Website: www.homebuildingshow.co.uk

Alpine Timber Frame Homes
Tel: 01807 500 765
Website: www.alpinetimberframe.com

Beaver Timber Company
Tel: 01631 720353
Website: www.beavertimber.co.uk
E-mail: TLH@beavertimber.co.uk

Country Homes Timber Frame Specialists
Tel: 01432 820660
Website: www.country_homes.org
E-mail: country_homes@yahoo.co.uk

Kingston Timber Frame
Tel: 01904 762589
Website: www.kingstontimberframe.co.uk

Finance

Buildstore
Tel: 0800 018 5740
Website: www.buildstore.co.uk/selfbuildfinance

Riley Associates
Tel: 01259 726650
Website: www.riley-associates.co.uk

Traditional Housing Bureau
Tel: 0134 472 5757
Website: www.housebuilder.org.uk

Insurance

Renovation insurance
Tel: 0845 230 9874
Website: www.renovationzone.com

Self-builder
Tel: 0800 018 7660
Website: www.self-builder.com

Self-Build Zone
Tel: 0845 230 9874
Website: www.selfbuildzone.com

Finding a plot

Online land and renovation database
Website: www.plotfinder.net

Buildstore
Website: www.buildstore.co.uk/plotsearch

Further reading

The Homebuilder's Handbook
Tel: 01527 834406

All About Self-Build
Tel: 01983 840310
Website: www.blackberry-books.co.uk

Building regulations

Building Regulations 2001, available from The Stationery Office
Tel: 0870 600 5522
Website: www.odpm.gov.uk

Surveyors

Royal Institution of Chartered Surveyors
Tel: 0870 333 1600
Website: www.rics.org

Underfloor heating

Advanced Floor Heating
Website: www.advancedfloorheating.com

Continental
Tel: 08456 023059
Website: www.continental-ufh.com

Invisible Heating Systems
Website: www.invisibleheating.co.uk

Nu-Heat UK Ltd
Tel: 01404 549770
Website: www.nu-heat.co.uk
E-mail: info@nu-heat.co.uk

UFHS(SW) Ltd
Website: www.underfloorheatingservices-sw.co.uk

Underfloor Heating Systems
Website: www.underfloorheatingsystems.co.uk

Warmup
Tel: 0845 345 2288
Website: www.warmup.co.uk

Winsbo
Tel: 01293 548512

Energy efficiency

Energy Efficiency Advice Centre
Website: www.energy-advice.co.uk

The Energy Saving Trust
Website: www.est.org.uk

The National Energy Foundation
Website: www.nef.org.uk/energyadvice/index.htm

Soundproofing

The Institute of Acoustics
Tel: 01727 848195
Website: www.ioa.org

Sound Reduction Systems
Tel: 01204 380074
Website: www.soundreduction.co.uk

Doors

The British Woodworking Federation
Website: www.bwf.org.uk

Cottage Joinery
Tel: 01568 720323

Doors of Distinction
Tel: 01202 872211
Website: www.doorsofdistinction.com

Fitzroy Joinery
Tel: 01752 334949
Website: www.fitzroy.co.uk

Real Door Company
Tel: 01462 451230
Website: www.realdoor.co.uk

Windows

The Glass and Glazing Federation
Tel: 0870 042 4255
Website: www.ggf.org.uk

Holdsworth Windows (specializes in replacement of period steel
windows and leaded lights)
Tel: 01608 661883
Website: www.holdsworthwindows.co.uk

Lamwood Limited
Tel: 01332 541540

The Original Box Sash Window Company
Tel: 01753 858196
Website: www.boxsash.com

QFS (sliding uPVC sash windows)
Tel: 0800 116611
Website: www.qfswindows.co.uk

The Sash Window Workshop (hand-built windows using traditional
methods)
Tel: 0800 597 2598
Website: www.sashwindow.com

Ventrolla (sash windows)
Tel: 0800 378 278
Website: www.ventrolla.co.uk

Architects

RIBA (Royal Institute of British Architects)
Tel: 020 7307 3700 (client services)
Website: www.ribafind.org

Architect Search
Tel: 0870 416 3378 (Design for Homes)
Website: www.architectsearch.co.uk

Thomas de Cruz
Tel: 020 8995 8100
Website: www.modernlondonhouse.com

Open Architecture
Tel: 020 8318 9700
Website: www.openarc.co.uk

Painters and decorators

Painting and Decorating Association
Tel: 024 7635 3776
Website: www.paintingdecoratingassociation.co.uk

Winona Peddar (handpainted designs)
Tel: 07850 438105

Interior design

Lorraine Johnson
Tel: 020 7622 1720

Really Linda Barker
Tel: 0845 4504025
Website: www.reallylindabarker.co.uk

Courses

BSY Group
Tel: 0800 731 9271
Website: www.bsygroup.co.uk
E-mail: info@bsygroup.co.uk

The Regent Academy
Tel: 0800 378 281
Website: www.regentacademy.com
E-mail: info@regentacademy.com

Technology

HTL Smart Systems (Home Technology Ltd)
Tel: 0845 021 2000
Website: www.htl-smartsystems.co.uk

Artex removal

Plaster 4U
Website: www.plaster-4u.com/artex

RemovAll
Website: www.paint-stripper.co.uk

SMH Products
Website: www.smhproducts.com/sales.htm

Ultimate Handyman
Website: www.ultimatehandyman.co.uk/decorating.htm

Tracing your home's history

The National Archives
Website: www.nationalarchives.gov/uk/house/history/guifr

UK and Ireland Genealogy (links to local history information)
Website: www.genuki.org.uk/big

Plumbers

Council for Registered Gas Installers (CORGI)
Tel: 0870 401 2300
Website: www.corgi-gas.co.uk

Institute of Plumbing
Tel: 01708 472791
Website: www.plumbers.org.uk

Courses

Skills Club
Tel: 020 8649 9340
Website: www.skillsclub.com

Carpenters

Institute of Carpenters
Tel: 0115 949 0641
Website: www.carpenters-institute.org

Roofers

National Federation of Roofing Contractors
Tel: 020 7436 0387
Website: www.nfrc.co.uk

Handymen

0800handyman
Tel: 0800 426 3962 (services available in London and a few other areas)
Website: www.0800handyman.co.uk

Power tools

Machine Mart
Tel: 0115 955 9999
Website: www.machinemart.co.uk

DIY stores

B&Q
Tel: 0845 222 1000
Website: www.diy.com

Homebase
Tel: 0870 900 8098
Website: www.homebase.co.uk

Ikea
Tel: 020 820 85600
Website: www.ikea.co.uk

Magnet
Tel: 01325 744344
Website: www.magnet.co.uk

MFI
Tel: 0870 609 5555
Website: www.mfi.co.uk

Wickes
Tel: 0870 6089001
Website: www.wickes.co.uk

Index

Index of advertisers